Radical Optimism

RADICAL OPTIMISM

Practical Spirituality
in an Uncertain World

BEATRICE BRUTEAU

SENTIENT PUBLICATIONS, LLC

Cover design by Kim Johansen, Black Dog Design

Library of Congress Cataloging-in-Publication Data available
at the Library of Congress

Printing History
First published by Crossroad Publishing Company, New York, 1996
Sentient edition ... 2002
Second Sentient printing ... 2004

Printed in Canada

10 9 8 7 6 5 4 3 2

SENTIENT PUBLICATIONS
A Limited Liability Company
1113 Spruce Street
Boulder, CO 80302
www.sentientpublications.com

Contents

Acknowledgments

The author and publisher gratefully acknowledge permission to reprint portions of this text which were previously published:

Chapter Four, "The Finite and the Infinite," appeared in *The Quest: A Quarterly Journal of Philosophy, Science, Religion & the Arts* 2/2 (Summer 1989): 64–73.

Portions of Chapter Six, "Heart of Jesus, Root of Reality," appeared in the articles "Entering the Heart of Jesus," *Cistercian Studies* 20 (1985): 116–30, and "In the Cave of the Heart: Silence and Realization," *New Blackfriars* 65 (July/August 1984): 301–19.

Chapter Eight, "Trinitarian Manifestation," appeared in *Cistercian Studies Quarterly* 24 (1989): 95–104, under the title "Trinitarian World."

Preface to the
Second Edition

The more troubled and difficult the world becomes, the more important it becomes to be optimistic. And the more deeply we need to root our optimism. When we cannot reasonably base it on the way things are going, we know that we have to base it in the ultimate reality of God. We know that it has to be radical.

Pierre Teilhard de Chardin said that we will not make the effort that is necessary to move us to the next stage of evolution, to form the world of the noosphere, the hyperpersonal, the world of global peace and friendship and prosperity, unless we believe it has a very good chance of succeeding. We need to be *optimistic*. Visions of utopias have a place in our thoughts and in our efforts because they activate the ideas and the desires that move us in those directions. In our personal lives and concerns, optimism makes a big difference, measurably improving our health and career success.

Mattie J.T. Stepanek, author of *Journey through Heartsongs*, says that "positive attitudes" impel us "towards the journey for world peace. And world peace, harmony, and confidence are essential for our future" [Poem 13]. Without confidence we may not have a future. And anyway, without confidence, who has the heart to go forward in living and to enjoy living? Confidence, optimism, is fundamentally necessary to true pleasure and happiness, to improvements, and to life itself.

This book is about a way of obtaining this radical optimism by means of contemplation. Contemplation means withdrawing attention from outward, objective, particular, and temporal concerns, and refocusing on inward, subjective, general and even eternal realities. This transcendent standpoint brings us into a deeper place with surer values and a more authentic selfhood. From this place we are also better able to deal with the temporal and particular. Essential to both the inward movement and the outward movement is an orientation we may call "purity of heart." Contemplation is not just an intellectual activity. It is also a moral and a devotional matter. Unless we have freed ourselves of violence, anger, vengefulness and vindictiveness, we will not be able to retire within. Unless we have detached from lust, greed, envy, and covetousness, we will not be able to refocus on the transcendent level. Unless we are energized by yearning for the divine as the Real and are willing to be embedded in it rather than making use of it, we will never find it.

People who are long-term practitioners of contemplation characteristically drop one local self-identification after another. They no longer see their personal reality limited to membership in this group rather than that. The whole truth about them is not summed up by a recital of what sex, race, nation, religion, social stratum they belong to. They experience themselves as being more real at a level that transcends all these classifications, and they simultaneously see other people at the same level of commonality. This view inevitably makes for peaceful and supportive relationships.

It is in this sense that contemplation necessarily involves metaphysics. Metaphysics is not an item in a New Age agenda but a branch of philosophy that studies what all beings have in common. It is the most general science. This is why the contemplative, after learning to quiet the mind sufficiently to withdraw it from the concerns of everyday particularity, focuses on the most far-reaching questions: the relation of the finite to the infinite, of the contingent to the necessary, of the temporal to the eternal. And, of these pairs themselves, we ask whether they are ineluctably polarized with respect to one another or whether they can be united in some way.

This metaphysical exploration is carried on in this book by means of familiar religious metaphors that invite the practicing contemplative to enter into a subjective perspective in which something universal can be seen. For instance, the meditation on "the heart of Jesus" is an exercise to help the meditator center into the core of Being, where both the infinite (divinity) and the finite (humanity) can be found in mutual indwelling. This kind of practice is proposed because the crucial transition in the contemplative process is not so much in what is seen as in the position from which it is seen. The subjective sense of existing shifts its "location" from a particular intersection of finite and contingent classes to the transcendent level of the infinite, necessary, and eternal. This is why the book concludes with the contemplation of "the communion of the saints," a deep awareness of the absolute universality of kinship among all those that are.

Contemplation thus both has a value in its own right, gaining insight into the nature of reality at its ultimate depth, and is fundamentally useful in dealing with our worldly problems. When we reach an impasse with some entity we are obliged to interact with, the only thing to do is back off and achieve a new perspective from a level transcendent to the problem level. When you do not identify with either of the adversaries, you can often see what assumptions are being made by each party—and sometimes by both. A situation of impasse is usually an indication that something is amiss with the assumptions. The contemplative practice can bring to consciousness what we have been taking for granted unconsciously. Once these assumptions have been exposed, they can be studied and reevaluated. Then a new effort can be made at resolving the problem. This can be a breakthrough experience for populations moving out of a worldview in which they believed themselves necessarily subject to some elite (based on assumptions about sex, race, wealth, religion, etc.). It is called for in all multi-cultural situations. It is relevant to any apparent "clash of civilizations." It is worth trying even in apparently irreconcilable quarrels over admittedly limited resources (such as the same piece of territory). When we seek the common ground, the more basic humanly shared values, we at least put ourselves in a more creative position for finding new approaches.

The present crisis, which is partly about culture and partly about economic control, needs to be seen in this context. There are "terrorists" abroad in the world, with dreadful weapons within their reach, and there is a System in place in the world which—almost unnoticed—has gained control over most of the fundamentals of life: food, jobs, welfare security, health and safety measures, protection (or not) of the environment, and information about what is going on. We need, urgently, to consider all over again, what is our life about, what values are important, which items serve others. Are human beings to serve economic growth, to the disruption of their livelihoods, their families, their right to know what they are eating and what events, significant to their lives, are taking place and who is making the decisions affecting them; or is the economy in service to human life, its well-being and happiness?

We need to find our way back to the very basic realities, truths, values. Contemplation is the road by which we may do this. We need to find the roots of our being: we need to be radical. And we need to do so in hope, even strong hope, for our condition is perilous. We will not have the will and the energy and the earnestness and the perseverance and the courage to engage the present crisis unless we believe that we can preserve our lives and our values. We need to believe that we can come into an arrangement whereby persons can manage freely to have voice in the conditions of their own lives. And that they can do it without infringing the parallel rights of other persons. We must want the well-being of all and of each in that all. Seeing such a vision and believing that it can be attained and committing ourselves to working toward it is what I mean by optimism — optimism that is rooted in deep reality and working out in love by skillful means.

Beatrice Bruteau
August 24, 2002

Preface

When we first started the Schola Contemplationis, I didn't know what the word *schola* really meant. I thought of it only as a school. We were forming a correspondence network for contemplatives—mostly laypeople, some religious; mostly Christians, but not all—who wanted to be in touch with others like themselves, to share their insights, to be reassured about their experiences, to feel the fellowship. We also had the idea that those who knew a little more about the contemplative life could teach those who were just entering upon it, and that the old hands could all teach one another. The Schola was to be a mutual, or cooperative, school in that sense.

But the Latin word *schola* comes from the Greek *scholē* which means "leisure." What an interesting discovery! Before you can teach, you must learn, and in order to learn, you must stop your busyness and hold still for a while. You must give yourself leisure to learn.

I saw then that there can be a sequence in the derived meanings of *schola,* and this book addressed to contemplatives reflects that sequence. First comes the leisure itself, the cessation of restless activity, the stillness and the silence. Then comes the learning, the instructive part, framing ideas that can help—"school" in our usual sense. Finally, we can have a "school" in the sense of a "school of thought," a community of shared insight, a body for concerted expression of the shared vision.

The vision I am trying to share has been called by a number of people "optimistic." Some of them are pleased on this account, some of them are not. The latter ask for more recognition of the pain with which life is filled, for acknowledgement of the difficulties of living a spiritual life, and for faith in the redemptive power of suffering. The former seem to get a lift from the "upbeat" attitude, find it new and refreshing, bringing to the front of the stage something that had been hovering in the wings, or perhaps present all the while unnoticed, painted on the backdrop.

My own notion about this is that of course we all know that life can show us an aspect of misery and malevolence and sorrow and horror. And because of this, it also can present us with doubt and perplexity and apparent absurdity, which is even worse. We feel that we could bear with the misery if we could just see some meaning. I am trying to contribute to the quest for meaning and the consequent alleviation of the misery. And I do not think that that can be done by constantly dwelling on how sinful or sorrowful or hard life is. Even when true, that isn't helpful. And I do not believe that it is the deepest truth.

The deepest truth is our union with the Absolute, Infinite Being, with God. That's the root of our reality. And it is from that root that my optimism is derived. That is why I decided to call it "radical optimism." The way to meaning is the path of perspective. We have to find the right angle from which to view our situation. I want to look at it from the root out into the branches, so to speak. It seems to me that situating ourselves somewhere on the periphery, amongst the twisting twigs and the fluttering leaves, gives us an inaccurate slant on things. It makes us identify with what I have called our "descriptions." But shift our sense of identity to the root, to our "real self," to the source of our being in God, and all looks very different.

Our model for this is Jesus, who could face torture and abandonment and still say, "Yet I am not alone, for the Father is with me. I have said this to you, that in me you may have peace. In the world you have tribulation; but be of good cheer, I have overcome the world" (John 16: 32–33). That's radical optimism. It's rooted in the Source of Being: "The Father is with me." Or, equally, "I am in the Father," "I am in the Source of Being." That is the point of view that "overcomes" the "tribulation" of "the world." And therefore we should "be of good cheer."

That is the deep truth of the matter, in my view. But this radical optimism is also practical. When the local realists tried to make Jesus acknowledge that Jairus's daughter was dead, he refused to listen, and told her father, "Do not fear, only believe" (Mark 5:36). How much more optimistic can you get than to believe that someone is not really dead when she has all the signs of being dead, and to believe that you can restore her to life and health? But that *believing,* that optimism, is the first and ineluctable step toward actually demonstrating what is held in the belief (Mark 11:23–24). If you say to yourself, this is hard to do, human nature is weak, we can't be expected to be like that, then you will have the same experience that Peter had when he tried to walk on the water. Being optimistic, he succeeded; but as soon as he began to doubt, to notice the difficulty, to think that maybe it couldn't be done, he began to sink. Jesus did not commend him for recognizing the outrageousness of his attempt, but scolded him for not holding on to his belief that he could do it (Matthew 14:28–31). Filling your mind, your imagination, your emotions, with the belief that you *can* do the good that you intend is the most powerful help you can bring to bear on actual accomplishment.

I believe this radical optimism is the good news of the gospel and I propose that we take it seriously. In this book I am proposing that we take it seriously with respect to the development of the contemplative life. Not that it is explicitly spoken of to any great extent. But this faith and mood clearly underlie and inform the whole approach. Spiritual practices on the contemplative path involve a certain amount of discipline and overturning of old habits, a willingness to shift viewpoints and accept different attitudes, the courage to think for oneself, to ask deeply probing questions and perhaps try unauthorized opinions, the perseverance to continue when success is not yet visible, and the heart to undertake one's contribution toward creatively "dancing the world."[1] There is a natural temptation to feel that all this, if not quite beyond our powers, is certainly very arduous and apt to lead to considerable discomfort and unpleasantness. So we tend to back off from the enterprise, or continuously to excuse ourselves because of the difficulty of the task. The virtue of radical optimism in this context is that it encourages us in the undertaking, sustains us in our efforts, reassures us that we can do it. It turns our thoughts and feelings in a positive direction, not letting them sink down in admissions of failure.

Optimism, like pessimism, tends to be a self-justifying outlook. The more pessimistic you are, the more you are likely to fail and thus justify your pessimism. And similarly, the more optimistic you are, the more apt you are to succeed and justify your optimism. However, my optimism is not merely pragmatic. I also believe that it is ultimately, metaphysically, true because of its being *radical* optimism, coming from the root of our being, securely held in the Absolute Being.

I have tried to explain how I see us rooted in the Absolute and expressing the Absolute in the world. That is the core of the contemplative life, so far as I can see at present. The heart of it is insight, or what I often call "realization." The preparation for this is the exercises of relaxation and faculty-training, and the sequents from it are what I have called "manifestation"—a kind of spontaneous overflow of goodness-filled being so powerful that it creates the world.

The realization rises up out of a mystical "leisure," when the world stops claiming your full attention for a moment out of time, for a divine sabbath. It gives you a seed that grows and branches and develops various sorts of "instruction." To the extent that the realization rings the truth-bell in other breasts, it forms a common ground, a dancing ground on which a community can, with delightful diversity, weave a collaborative pattern. So it may be said to be a "contemplative school," a Schola Contemplationis.

ONE

♦

Leisure

One of the attractive aspects of the contemplative life, we fondly think, is that it is a life of leisure. Peaceful, without stress, it floats softly through charming landscapes in slow motion. Since there is nothing pressing us that has to be done, we are free to reflect and enjoy. If we think we want to be contemplatives, one of the reasons may be that we think we want such a life of leisure.

But what really is leisure? And how do we really feel about leisure? For many of us "leisure" actually raises difficulties: difficulties about conceiving it, about justifying it, about wanting it, and about practicing it.

We are busy people. Our time is highly structured and totally filled. We have deadlines to meet, schedules to keep. We measure our lives in terms of times: years, semesters, quarters, months, weeks, days, hours, minutes. We automatically think of our life as measured. It is part of our taken-for-granted image of how things are.

We are jealous and possessive about our time. It is perhaps our most precious possession. "I can give you five minutes," says the important executive. "Time is money," say the banker and the manufacturer. "I have to budget my time," active and intelligent people say, "I have to set priorities."

On the other hand, we are ourselves enslaved by time. We are pressured and harassed by our need to force many activities into small amounts of time. There are so many things that we must get done. If we do not do them, we feel guilty. And indeed, in many cases things do fall apart if our task is not accomplished in time. We've structured our lives that way.

Punctuality, like cleanliness, we feel, is next to godliness. Waiting is intolerable; to keep someone waiting is offensive, discourteous. We have an injunction against "wasting time" that inhibits our capacity to enjoy idle moments. Time spent doing nothing is time lost, time without value. Those of us who feel this way (mostly in cultures that use clocks) have so elevated our cultural dispositions toward time into moral virtues, that when we make contact with individuals or cultures which are more casual about time, we tend to regard them as impolite or uncivilized.[1]

We are uneasy with unfilled time. Leisure, for us, is another set of activities, often as pressured as those they replace. Even our playing is organized and competitive. If we travel, we have to meet our goal of so many miles each day and be sure we have covered all the points of interest at the place visited. Leisure activities have become big business. People have to be kept occupied. We can't bear simply to be still and do nothing. This is why we laugh nervously at the Zen joke: "Don't just do something; sit there!"

Not doing, not measuring time, not measuring life by time, not measuring people by how they measure time—all these are difficulties for many of us, even those of us who think we want the life of leisure, the contemplative life. How many contemplative monasteries are run rigidly by the clock? It is hard to free ourselves from deeply embedded cultural habits.

And yet we suffer from our way of relating to time. "Hurry sickness" is now a recognized phenomenon in medical circles.[2] It includes high blood pressure, ulcers, tension headaches, Type A personalities who drive themselves to heart attacks, edgy tempers that spoil personal relationships, haste that makes mistakes, rushing about that takes the joy out of life.

We may need to back away from our lives a bit and ask ourselves, What is our conception of time? How do we see time? see ourselves in time? value time? What have we taken for granted without considering that perhaps it could be seen otherwise?

Albert Einstein remarked that the normal adult never asks fundamental questions about space-time because we assume that whatever there was to ask has already been asked and answered long ago and now forms the background for everything else that we experience. But Einstein himself developed unusually slowly as a child—he did not speak until he was two years old—and so, he says, "I only began to wonder about space and time when I was already grown up. In consequence, I probed deeper into the problem than an ordinary child would have done."[3]

Now this is what the contemplative is called to do: to become again as a child, wondering about the fundamental things, not taking any answers for granted, but having an adult's intelligence and ability to realize that there may be various answers.

Let us do this with respect to time, because this question will underlie many others, and the disposition of leisure that we may attain will enable us to do other things. The contemplative life has always required an attitude of leisure, and leisure has often resulted in contemplation.

What is an attitude of leisure? Does it really require absolutely free time, time in which one is not doing anything at all? To answer the last question first, it does not require that one be totally unoccupied, and it is, of course, a good thing that it does not, for we all have to do a good many things. However, among the things that we have been taking for granted may be the belief that we really have to do all these things. If we were to make a list of our activities and then ask ourselves seriously whether we really need do each of them, we might be amazed to find how many could be stricken from the list.

What is most important, though, is the attitude and disposition of leisure. To get a feel for the attitude of leisure, I think we will do well to consider the biblical notion of the sabbath rest. Notice that it is not just a practical and sensible and compassionate practice, but it is a way of relating to the holiness of God and of entering into the secret of the divine life:

> "Remember the sabbath day, to keep it holy. Six days you shall labor, and do all your work; but the seventh day is a sabbath to the Lord your God; in it you shall not do any work." (Exodus 20:8)

I want to develop two thoughts out of this text: one has to do with holiness as wholeness, the opposite of fragmentation, and the other has to do with not laboring.

Our usual experience of time—and consequently of all our life—is a fragmented experience. Yet we know, if we have any acquaintance with the spiritual life, even if only by hearsay (i.e., by the traditional teachings), that the underlying Reality is a continuous Wholeness, a Unity beyond any possibility of division. This is part of the insight of monotheism in the Abrahamic religions[4] and is the foundation also of Hindu and Buddhist spiritual systems. Both the East and the West have expressed this Wholeness, and the transcendence of time which is one aspect of Wholeness, by speaking of the Ultimate as unchangeable.

In the personalist context of Judaism this is represented dramatically as God's loyalty. God is a person, and a person is essentially a free will, but God's will does not change. Once having plighted his troth, God is steadfast in love.

God's love, God's will, God's personal selfhood is one Wholeness, unfragmented. A fragmented will can be loyal one day and disloyal the next. A fragmented will can change over time. But God's will is integral, utterly reliable, immovable, eternal. The biblical context of "The Eternal" is not cosmic and metaphysical, like the Greek or Hindu philosophical notions (which are also true of God), but is personal and volitional. It means that God will never forsake us. "His great love is without end . . . and the faithfulness of the Lord endures for ever" (Psalm 117–18).

We are called to realize ourselves as children of God. Children inherit their parents' qualities. Therefore we are to realize our own participation in eternity. And to help us do this we have the commandment, "Keep holy the sabbath day." The sabbath is the sacramental representative of God's eternity, and we are to keep it whole, unfragmented.

What we call the "commandments" of God are really statements of revelation and empowerment. They tell us what we need to do to fulfill ourselves, and they promise that we are able to do what they indicate. This one says that we can keep the sabbath of the Lord's rest whole, without a break. We can keep it *all the time.* All the sacraments we have enable us to contact a Reality that is *always* present, although the sacrament itself stands apart from everyday experience in order to call our attention to itself and to the Reality that it mediates. Similarly the sabbath. It is not really one time among other times, but the underlying eternity, which *is,* "all the time."

What does it mean to keep the sabbath whole, without break? It means to rest our central consciousness steadily, without wavering, on God, the Wholeness, the Holy One, the Eternal. "Thou dost keep him in perfect peace whose mind is stayed on Thee" (Isaiah 26:3). This is the contemplative state. This is the same as "praying without ceasing." This is coming into realization of the truth that is the transcendent Wholeness, the ultimate Unity.

Our central consciousness is not our peripheral consciousness. We, like God, are persons, and a person is essentially a free will. Our will is to be the match and image of God's will, that is, steadfast, without fluctuation, loyal, committed. But our central consciousness is also our deepest mind, that is, our widest context, our most comprehensive insight, our most basic assumption. And here we must be vigilant and keep awake to catch ourselves when we are being tempted to believe in fragmentation.

We *can* keep our consciousness in the divine Eternity, without break; we can realize the underlying ultimate Wholeness of Reality. This is not to say that it is something that we produce out of our operations on the natural plane, but to say that it is not something impossible, something that ought not to be expected. If we are to realize, we must first believe: that is, we must trust and rely on the enabling commandment. And then we must permit ourselves to find our base and our center in that sense of eternity and wholeness by not insisting on believing in fragmentation as the ultimate Reality. In a way, this is the whole of the spiritual life, but in the present context I want to focus on how this relates to our sense of time, so that we can relax our tendency to rush, hurry, be tense, try to accomplish and produce.

In sabbath consciousness we don't have to rush or accomplish or produce. In sabbath consciousness we are not to labor. Labor is what is done on the six days, that is, in the finite and temporal world. It consists of moving things in relation to one another with a view to producing something, accomplishing something by our efforts. We exercise our natural talents and abilities and energies on the things of this world. In terms of the spiritual life, we exercise our natural spiritual talents of intelligence and good will and affectivity. Labor means trying to get closer to God by *doing things,* both exteriorly and interiorly.

Alan Watts says somewhere that all these spiritual exercises have to be done in order to convince us that they are both impotent and unnecessary. They will not "produce" union with God, and they don't *have* to, because our being united with God is something God does, not something we do, or, if you prefer, because we were always united with God and cannot not be. But initially, and in our hurry and busyness about many things, we don't see that. We think that we must attend ceremonies, practice virtues, perform ascetical exercises, accept the correct doctrines and pray the right prayers, in order to attain an intimate relationship with God. So we do these things. And they do help. They correct our moral life and bring our human energies into an ordered and quieted condition in which we may become open to the great truth. But the most interesting thing that they do is that they eventually frustrate us completely and convince us of their utter uselessness for attaining the ultimate goal. We must labor all these six days in order to break out of the consciousness that believes in the necessity and efficacy of such labor. "But the seventh day is a sabbath to the Lord your God; in it you shall not do any work."

St. Teresa of Avila speaks of this contrast of our working and God fulfilling under the image of watering a garden. The gardener labors in various ways to carry water to the garden, but in the end God waters the garden without any labor on the gardener's part by sending rain. This is the ultimate truth about our spiritual life, about our prayer life. It is not our labors, represented by the six days of work, that produce real prayer. Real prayer is present in God's sabbath.

Now, a certain part of our consciousness already knows this and can rest in this knowledge, even while we continue with our secular and spiritual labors. The *attitude* of leisure is the attitude of confidence that trusts in the commandment to keep the sabbath and to rest in it, and therefore not to identify one's deepest reality with the works and labors in which one engages.

This attitude gives a sense of release and freedom, even while we continue to be faithful and persevering in our responsibilities. The deepest part of our consciousness knows that we live in eternity, that sabbath consciousness is the underlying consciousness on which the six working days develop their finite and relative forms.

Relaxing Ego-Consciousness

This deepest part of our consciousness, which various spiritual writers call by various names—Thomas Merton, for instance, calls it "the true Self"—has to be distinguished from our ego-consciousness, and we will be saying a great deal about that later on. This distinction and the shifting of our experienced center of gravity, or sense of selfhood, from the ego to the true self, constitutes the core of the spiritual enterprise.

Ego-consciousness is that which judges everything in our experience according to whether it is good or bad *for me* as a private, separate individual, rather than according to whether it is good or bad in itself, or within the context of some greater whole, or from God's point of view. It is the consciousness that identifies us with our description, with all the things that can be said about us in comparison with others—that we are taller or handsomer or smarter or richer, or of the opposite sex or the adverse political party, or inside or outside the right church, or more extroverted or less sensitive, or whatever. It is the consciousness that makes us feel the need to insist on getting our way and defending our existence and our description. In short, by ego-consciousness we see ourselves as separated beings, fragments that relate to other fragments in terms of efforts to obtain some advantage.

One of the characteristics of ego-consciousness is the way it sees time. Since it identifies itself in terms of its descriptions, it always sees time as either past or future. When we think of ourselves as the ego, as our description in comparison with others, we think either of how we have been or of how we shall be or hope we shall be. If we think of ourselves as ego, right now, we can see that what comes to mind, if we analyze it a little, is either a memory or an anticipation. Our whole sense of ourselves as ego-description is made up of such compounds of memories and desires, of the past and the future.

This fact, when we carefully observe and understand it, is a clue to how to find the true self and get out of ego-consciousness: stop thinking of yourself in terms of past and future. Because the ego is a description, it has to be a set of comparisons; because it is a set of comparisons, the various items to be compared have to *hold still*, keep whatever nature they have that is being compared. Ego-consciousness is thus like a view of still photographs. But a still photograph has to be of the past—or of the future: we think of the future exactly the same way we think of the past, only adding the remark that this slice of past hasn't happened yet.

Now, if we eliminate past and future, we eliminate comparisons of descriptions and thus ego-consciousness. What is left? The strict present and the real self, without any description, what spiritual writers sometimes call "the naked soul." You can test this by actual experience. By keeping your consciousness quietly and simply just on the present moment, you will see that memory, anticipation, guilt, and anxiety all disappear. Neither is there any fantasy in a consciousness stayed on the present moment. It has to be perfectly realistic. It is living in the past or in the future that is fantasy, that is unrealistic. But that is what our ego-consciousness does, and it finds no peace there. The present moment is the intersection of eternity with time, and when our consciousness is stayed on this, it rests and finds peace, because it is released from the fantasies of the ego and is in touch with reality.

Don't misunderstand. This is not to say that we should never think of the past or future, that we shouldn't study history or make plans for times to come. What we are talking about is how we think of our own deepest being, our sense of who we really are, and of where all reality is ultimately rooted. The reality of God appearing in live action is to be found only in this sense of the present moment, because it alone is living, real, dynamic. One of the things that the contemplative learns by experience is that the Eternal, the Infinite, the Absolute, the One, coexists with the temporal, the finite, the relative, the many. Thus, for instance, Jesus says, "My Father works until now, and I work," while the Epistle to the Hebrews says, "There remains a sabbath rest for the people of God; for whoever enters God's rest also ceases from his labors as God did from his. Let us therefore strive to enter that rest" (Hebrews 4:9).

But how shall we "strive" to enter this rest, since we have just said that striving doesn't produce what we seek and is, in any case, unnecessary? The author of Hebrews has an answer, drawn from Psalm 95. Psalm 95 speaks of those of whom God says "They shall never enter my rest," because "they always go astray in their hearts and they have not known my ways." Therefore, the psalm urges: "Today, when you hear His voice, harden not your hearts" (Hebrews 3:7–4:7).

"Today"—that is, right now, in the present moment. Not some time in the future. "When you hear His voice"—the interface of the eternal with the temporal, a real contact, in the present moment, for which we must listen. Listening is a nonproductive, contemplative activity, a kind of striving not to strive, for self-striving would make noise and prevent us from hearing. "Harden not your hearts"—that is the chief thing. Be still and be open.

We *do* by not doing and by undoing. This is why we begin with leisure, the relaxing of the sense of time, of the sense of ego-selfhood, of the sense of fragmentation. I think most of the spiritual life is really a matter of relaxing—of what

Meister Eckhart called *Gelassenheit*—of letting go, ceasing to cling, ceasing to insist on our way, ceasing to tense ourselves up *for* this or *against* that, living by the fruits of the tree of consciousness of private good and evil.

Let us start now to attend to relaxing, first our bodies, in the usual sense, just unwinding after our work. Then our minds and emotions. Instead of trying to force ourselves to feel this or not feel that, trying to control ourselves by tension, we should rather relax our feelings, just as we would relax a tense muscle. The Hindus say that if you look at your mind and emotions as if at the surface of a lake, you will see your agitation as rough waves. But if you continue just to look at them and notice that *you* who are looking *are not* the agitated waves, then gradually those waves will subside. They will damp down, smooth out, and after a while the surface of the lake will be calm. Once the water is calm, it also becomes transparent. Then you can look down through it, clear to the bottom. When our mind becomes clear and transparent, we can perceive what lies at its bottom, its foundation: it is the peace of God, the divine Eternity. Then the mind rests happily in this state, even while we go about our business, doing the things that need to be done.

We can verify the words of the prophet Isaiah: "Everyone who keeps the Sabbath and does not profane it, and holds fast to my covenant—these I will bring to my holy mountain, and make them joyful in my house of prayer" (Isaiah 56:6–7). That is the fundamental disposition of leisure which makes possible the experience of contemplation.

TWO

♦

Stillness

O that today you would hearken to his voice!
Harden not your hearts. . . .

Psalm 95: 7–8

The most important thing in initiating a contemplative attitude toward life is being still and open. I see it as involving various levels of relaxation and silence, the kinds of not-doing that are so essential to the contemplative life.

Hearts can be hardened—or "tensed up"—in the same way that muscles can, and as a matter of fact the two things usually go together. If you will notice, any time that you have taken up an attitude that amounts to some kind of hardness of heart toward God's voice (a resentment toward someone, or anger, or wounded self-love, or jealousy, or desire for revenge, or contempt, or refusal to be generous), you will find your muscles are tight too. And on the other hand, if you can get really well relaxed in body, it is practically impossible to hold any of these attitudes of inner tension. If the tension comes into your mind again, the muscles will tense up, too.

It is also true that when you adopt an attitude of generosity, unselfishness, trust, rejoicing in another's good, love, respect, fellowship, then your muscles tend to relax. And if you can relax them first, then it is also easier to find these outgoing dispositions in your soul.

Relaxing the Body

So the first step in stillness is, very prosaically and humbly, relaxation of bodily tensions. Insofar as these are tied to emotional tensions, the two will have to relax together; but we may be able to get at the body more easily. This is a whole program of learning and unlearning and is not achieved overnight. You may be tempted to believe that *your* habits of tension cannot be transformed. But since they are habits and habits are learned, tension habits can be unlearned and relaxation habits can be learned. We may acknowledge our temptation to believe in the difficulty, but we do not focus on the difficulty, because focusing on difficulty and talking about it is itself a tension-inducing practice. (It may also be a way of excusing ourselves for an incomplete resolve to enter upon a more healthful path.) Instead, we talk about our capacity to experience relaxation and encourage an expectation to experience relaxation because that picture in the mind is itself a help toward relaxing.

There are many methods available now for unlearning tension habits and replacing them with "appropriate tone" habits—the right and comfortable level of tension for the particular situation. I am not going to discuss them here because that would be a whole book in itself and because each individual must experiment and find a method individually suitable. However, this issue must be dealt with at the beginning of any contemplative enterprise because it is basic to all else that follows. "Letting go" is a central theme in the spiritual life, and we can start to practice it at the place where we most obviously run into it, our bodily tensions and their emotional counterparts.

Three principles are important here, as well as throughout the course of contemplative development, it seems to me: (1) *Understand* what is going on and how our own system operates, in this case how our bodily states and emotional states are related and how habits are formed and can be changed. (2) Have a *wholehearted determination* to move into the new state, not a halfhearted or tentative attitude; in this case, really decide to give up tension attitudes and commit yourself without reservation to doing whatever you have selected as the means to learn the new way. (3) *Practice.* Practice every day, every hour, no exceptions, no excuses.

The contemplative intends to tame the body, keep it healthy and calm and well regulated. Traditional contemplative practices for this may include vigorous exercise (sometimes hard work), a plain diet, avoidance of stimulating or depressing chemicals, a pacifying routine and rhythmic regularity in external life fitted to the rhythms of nature, and protection from many of the pressures and tensions of secular society. We may not be able so to control our environment as to enjoy the pacifying rhythms and the freedom from secular pressures, though we can do some things even in these areas and we can compensate with interior attitudes, as we will see later. But there is hardly anything to prevent us from avoiding tobacco, alcohol, other drugs (even caffeine, which often isn't counted), enjoying a healthful diet for our particular weight and condition, and taking appropriate exercise.

The next step is to keep the body still, in two senses: to keep silence by not speaking, and to hold still in a prayer or meditation posture, without moving. The idea is to make tensions and distractions cease. One learns to sit still. Breathing, the fundamental rhythm of the body, becomes quiet and regular. This, in turn, tends to quiet the nervous system and the endocrine system, so that the body is not agitated or excited. In meditation we become balanced between relaxation and alertness, by letting go both our restlessness and our drowsiness. Meditation is itself balanced by work and physical exercise. Thus, guided by good hygiene, the body comes under an increasing degree of control, so that it moves gracefully, rests quietly in dignified postures, tires less easily, becomes supple and agile, and enjoys improved health.

This requires persevering practice and a disposition neither to be angry with oneself for failure, nor to excuse and justify oneself, nor to give in to discouragement. We must say to ourselves, Everybody who tries to do this goes through the same sort of experiences that I'm having. There's nothing wrong with me; this is par for the course. I'm retraining myself to do something different from what I'm used to doing. But when I have accustomed myself to it, I am going to feel much better! It can be learned, plenty of people have learned it, and I can too!

Silence

Relaxing our compulsion to talk can be very illuminating to us. We will be obliged to ask ourselves whence this urgency arises. What insecurity about our existence makes us want to chatter about trivia? Do we have to reassure ourselves that we are not isolated? that we are living in a common world? Do we need to draw the attention of other people to ourselves, as if their recognition of us helps sustain us? Do we keep distracting ourselves by a running commentary on superficial events lest we fall back into a realization of the fundamental mystery of our existential situation?

When we undertake to keep silence for a given period, as for instance on a silent retreat for a weekend or for eight days, if the silence is a problem for us, we can pay attention to what *kind* of discomfort we are experiencing, what we feel we are lacking, what we are afraid of. We can notice what we do to compensate for the speech-silence. Do we try to catch others' eyes and smile or wink or make gestures? Do we try to stay in sight of others? Do we read books or engage in imaginary conversations?

Or, do we find the silence tranquillizing, liberating, even exhilarating? Do we instinctively keep our eyes to ourselves, go off alone in the woods, spend time gazing out over the landscape? Do we find that even our usual internal conversation is quieting down? Perhaps all sorts of interior movements are coming to a halt, settling into stillness and repose. And we ourselves seem to be drawing to the center, as if to the lowest and most natural place to come to rest.

What about our prayer? Is God just somebody to talk to? Are we pouring out to God all the words we are holding in, not speaking to fellow human beings? That's not silence. See what happens if you stop talking to God, too. Be vividly in God's presence, but don't say anything. And don't imagine God talking to you, either. Both of you be quiet, just be together and enjoy it. What happens?

The practice of silence forces us to deeper levels of reality. Deprived of distraction, we must either panic or come to a new kind of authenticity. To avoid the horror of existential isolation, we must open ourselves to experience our union with the natural world, with the human world, and with God, without the cover-up that prattling had afforded us. Like the proto-amphibian stranded by a receding flood, we must learn to breathe in a new medium. We must learn to breathe *trust*, the unspoken communion.

Relaxation of Sense Desires

This leads to the next level of stillness and openness, the relaxation of desire. A life of regular habits and the deepened authenticity released by silence reduce the problem of disordered desires considerably. The desires of the senses are more teachable and more changeable, I think, than we often give them credit for being. New tastes can be acquired and old ones forsaken sometimes in a matter of days, and by almost everyone in a matter of weeks, if there is the will to have it so.

It is true that this is easier for some people than for others, and some may need the help of professionals or of some special program. The three principles mentioned above are important here: Understand how you work; that in itself gives you some transcendence of the problem, some psychic distance from it and power over it. Thoroughly resolve to relinquish whatever is under consideration. Don't say, Well, I'll give it a try. Especially don't say, I've tried it before, and it didn't work; I can't do it. Never give yourself negative reinforcement for something you want to be rid of. And then practice whatever method of release of desire you have decided to use. Practice with patience, good humor, and confidence.

The most important thing is this: Don't represent to yourself what you are doing as difficult. Don't keep saying how hard it is, don't remember your failures. Don't imagine the project as a tremendous task, a huge effort. Be like a weight lifter who deliberately concentrates on the bar and imagines it to be light as a feather. We are surrounded by people who want us to be "realistic" by directing our attention to how difficult it is to bring ourselves into a healthful, happy, and holy balance. But this isn't *helpful*! We must turn away from such "realism" of the world we are leaving, toward the reality of the world we are entering.

If we want to obtain contemplative quiet on the level of our sense desires, it is essential that we begin by believing that it can be done. Everything in our secular culture encourages us to believe that we must be controlled by our sense desires, indeed that we *are* our sense desires. And, unfortunately, many voices in the religious culture also tell us that custom is very strong and that the flesh has to be combatted and struggled with. The images are of great difficulty, tension, unlikely success. But the gospel tells us that whatever we ask for, we must believe *can be done*. "Truly, I say to you, whoever says to this mountain, 'Be taken up and cast into the sea,' and does not doubt in his heart, but believes that what he says will come to pass, it will be done for him. Therefore I tell you, whatever you ask in prayer, believe that you receive it, and you will" (Mark 11:23–24). That belief is the first step in obtaining what we seek. And if we believe it can be done with a fair degree of ease—think of that weight-lifter!—it will be done unto us according to our faith.

Is it important to be able to relax our sense desires? Why bother? The spiritual desire of the contemplative is usually framed in one of two ways: (1) the desire to find the ultimate truth and reality and to live in conformity with that, free from any illusion; or (2) the desire to give oneself without qualification to God in perfect obedience and full love. But if one is controlled by unnecessary sense desires, one will not be free in one's own consciousness and will not be able to commit oneself without reservation. One will always have to say, "As long as I don't have to give up so-and-so." But this is incompatible with the contemplative's own most comprehensive desire, which is to be totally integrated, thoroughly one, altogether intent on only one thing, the Ultimate Reality and Value.

> One thing have I asked of the Lord, that will I seek after, that I may dwell in the house of the Lord all the days of my life, to behold the beauty of the Lord, to enjoy His presence in His temple. (Psalm 27)

That is the contemplative vocation. We are to behold the beauty of the Lord, and it is the silencing of our distractions and private demands on life that makes this possible. When we are absorbed in our insistences that life be this way or that, that we have something or be spared something, then we cannot be aware of and appreciate the beauty of the Lord. Concern with our own noisy desires interferes with our enjoyment of all the things in the world, the special qualities of other people, the variety of creation in all its aspects. When our own personality is busy sounding off, we automatically narrow our perception to just what is going on here, and so miss everything else that is going on in God's wonder-filled world.

I think we should notice that what interferes with our living a contemplative life is not the busy, noisy, confused, demanding, harassing world in which we must earn our living and care for our families. We like to blame this environment, but that is not really the source of the disquiet. Even if we could go to the country, have nothing much to do and no threats to our comfort, we would take our own noisiness with us. We would make problems out of trivialities—as happens in contemplative monasteries where the opportunities for distress have (by the standards of the rest of the world) been considerably diminished. Let us recognize where our problem is truly lodged and then confidently release it. We can be peaceful, even in the midst of the demands of contemporary life, because what is really pressuring us is the insistence of our own demands. Once we are convinced that these demands can be *let go,* everything will begin to look very different.

Personality Demands

Everything I have said here about *sense desires* applies also to *personality desires:* desires for approval and admiration, desires to be preferred and advanced, to succeed, to have power or wealth, to dominate others, to have things go our way, not to be inconvenienced or humiliated, desires to have the last word, to defend ourselves, to think well of ourselves, or even, perversely, to think ill of ourselves. All these desires which ordinarily cry out all day long to be heard and answered, all have to be quieted. We have to be able to say with the psalmist, "I have calmed and quieted my soul, like a child quieted at its mother's breast; like a child that is quieted is my soul" (Psalm 131).

How does one do this? Again, we begin with understanding. What is to be quieted here is our *insistence* on having things our own way. This is what causes our suffering, as the Buddha pointed out, and this is what prevents us from being open to God and letting the divine life move in and through us.

A distinction has to be made carefully here. It is a distinction between *wishing* and *willing*.[1] I suggested that we not insist on having our circumstances and our experiences be some certain way. But this does not mean that if life can be improved, in a way consistent with the general welfare, we should not seek it.

For instance, if we are concerned over a matter of social justice, or protection of the environment, or prevention of nuclear war, then we may well judge that we have a duty to make every effort to realize our goals. We do not simply consent to matters being as they presently are. But even as we take steps to bring an important ideal into actuality, we need not murmur and complain that this or that effort of ours turned out as it did, or resent the slowness with which the changes come.

Our interior disposition should be a firm *will* that justice be done and that the situation be changed as soon as possible—and we should take all the actual concrete steps to do this—but at the same time, we need not indulge in *wishing* that things were, at any given moment, other than as they are. If you will observe the two interior acts closely, you will see the difference.

Wishing acknowledges the expected continuation of the undesired situation. It admits that we believe we cannot change it. We look, as it were, to someone or something else to change it for us. But we look vaguely, not toward some specific helper. Wishing leaves us feeling dispirited, without energy. It does not incite us to action. We moan, but we do not move.

Willing, on the other hand, is the first step in actually changing the situation. It commits us to belief that the situation can be changed and that it can be changed by us (perhaps with unknown helpers). This relieves tension and brings peace, because we have already turned our face toward the good that we are determined to bring into being. The sense of peace releases energy which is focused by the commitment, and productive action results.

So, stilling our personality desires, our insistence that we personally be pleased, is necessary for contemplation, but does not mean that we are not to will, and to act for, the improvement of our common life.

But now, getting back to the personality demands that we judge should be let go, how do we manage to do it? How can I just "release" my need for approval, my desire for success, my instinct to dominate others, get my way, have the last word, always be right, and so on? The very enumeration of the needs points to the answer. We evidently feel that our selfhood is very insecure and has to be defended and augmented by these means. Is that true? Is our selfhood that tentative and contingent? No matter what spiritual tradition we are following, the answer is no. All traditions tell us that we are safe. Either they say that God loves us, sustains us in being and well-being and will never forsake us; or they say that the very nature of our *real* selfhood is such that it cannot suffer injury and is already (though secretly) perfect. Obviously, we don't believe what our traditions tell us, because we keep trying to find what we imagine to be more advantageous positions for ourselves in the personality world.

Let us ask ourselves. What is it that I really want? What am I trying to obtain by my demands that my personality be dominant—or at least be protected, not humiliated, and be able to "feel good about" itself? And clearly, what we want is to be free from worry about the well-being of the self. We want a state in which we won't have to make ourselves tense and anxious by demands such as these. The way to release, then, is to trace back the demand, to see what it is really, finally, seeking, what we really want. And when that is clearly seen, we can turn to our tradition, whatever it is, and hear it say, But you already *have* that. There's nothing to worry about. Even if human beings don't give you the respect you want, God does. Doesn't that mean more? Even if your phenomenal human personality isn't in the most advantageous position relative to other human personalities, your *real* self isn't relative! It doesn't have to struggle for recognition and a good position. The only "you" that really matters is quite safe and in good condition. Believe that, relax, and enjoy life.

There is more to it than that, of course, and we will continue to discuss it, but that's a beginning. We need also to study stilling the imagination and the mind, and I will discuss those in connection with meditation in the following chapter. For the rest of this chapter, I want to present some words of Jesus and a way of being with Jesus that enable us to relax into this state of quietness.

Help from the Teacher

In John 16:33 Jesus says, "I have said these things to you that in me you may have peace. In the world you have tribulation; but be of good cheer, I have overcome the world." If you look up some of these words in a Greek dictionary, it sometimes helps you to have a deeper appreciation of the possibilities of the text. In this case, the word for "tribulation" is *thlipsin*. It means "pressure," basically, hence oppression, or affliction. That's something we can relate to: we have pressures on us in our world, pressures from outside us and pressures from inside us.

"But be of good cheer," says Jesus. The word is *tharseite,* "be confident, feel secure." "I have overcome the world"— *nenikeka,* "I have won the victory, conquered, prevailed over." So what he is saying is, "You are under a lot of pressure in the world, but be confident and feel secure, because I have won out over the world."

And in Matthew 11:28 he says, "Come to me, all you who labor and are heavy laden, and I will give you rest." Labor: *kopiontes,* to work until you are weary and exhausted. "I will give you rest": *anapauso,* literally, "I will make it cease." It means "I will give you relief" in the sense of relief *from* something, by *stopping* whatever it is that you are to be relieved from: "I will relieve you," meaning "I'll stop the pain," or "I'll lift the burden," or "When I come on duty, you can stop working."

Put together, the two texts say: "I have stopped the pressures of the world and I can give you relief, too."

How? This is answered in the following verse, Matthew 11:29: "Take my yoke upon you and learn from me; for I am gentle and lowly in heart." The word now rendered "gentle" in the RSV used to be translated "meek." In Greek it is *praus.* It means "calm, with passions tamed." A possible image evoked by this text is that of training draft animals. If an unruly and high-spirited animal is put into a double yoke together with a tamed and stable animal of even temperament, the unruly one will gradually calm down too and learn to be quiet and obedient.

The suggestion is that all these things are connected: peace, victory over the pressure and afflictions of the world, being yoked together with Jesus who is calm, with passions tamed, and the act of "making it cease." The key to it seems to be this idea of being yoked together with Jesus and learning from him who is already quiet and free from passions.

Another gospel story may be pertinent here. It is the story of Martha and Mary (Luke 10:38–42). Martha is said to be anxious and troubled about many things. Let us say in our context that she wants to be a contemplative, and she is trying to relax her body and her nervous system and breathe properly and keep silence and sit still and give up coffee, cigarettes, and second desserts, and not snap at her children and not resent her colleague's getting the promotion instead of herself, and so on. It's like one person trying to get dinner for a crowd: while she is making the salad, the soup boils over, and while she's cleaning that up, the rolls burn!

Jesus has the answer. You don't need a seven-course dinner, he says. "One [dish] is all that is necessary" (Luke 10:42). Just make spaghetti, and then come sit down with me, as Mary's doing. After all, he jestingly points out, Mary's already having a whole feast!

The Hindus have a word for this: *upāsana*. It means to sit down near. It is what one does when the right teacher has been found. What happens then? Is it just a matter of listening and taking notes, and being ready to recite? What really happens with that kind of teacher is that one catches something. It is a kind of contagion. It doesn't necessarily pass in the words but exudes from the teacher's being in some way. The teacher has found peace and freedom and truth. Those who live near the teacher and pick up this tenor and rhythm and style and inner form of life will be helped to find *their* peace and freedom and truth.

We may speak of it as "entraining." Entrainment is the phenomenon of two rhythmic beings gradually altering their phases until they are locked together in the same rhythm. Pendulums hanging on the same wall will do it; insects that chirp or blink will do it; even two human beings talking to each other will do it.[2]

And Christian contemplatives who meditate on Jesus can do it. What we think of, we tend to become. If we fill our minds and especially our imaginations with the life-rhythm of Jesus, we will find that the unruly desires and insistences cease.

Our part in this work is not to fight it. We do not have to undertake the job piecemeal as I described Martha as doing, trying to force out each indulgence in turn and getting anxious about them all. Only one thing is necessary: we just relax into the contemplation of the man Jesus, absorb his peacefulness, his tamed soul, his freedom, his unity within himself, and his absolute devotion to God. We let go distracting thoughts and turn to him as more interesting, more desirable. No force, no stress, no strain, no tension. All successful contemplation is relaxed contemplation.

This is being open to having our desires changed, our lifestyle changed, our tastes and pleasures changed. If we resist and do not want them changed—if we harden our hearts—then, of course, we can't expect anything to happen. But if we relax and let the influence of Jesus' life and presence work on us, then gradually the rhythm and reality of his being will engulf us, we will be entrained by him, our heart will beat, so to speak, in unison with his.

So let us take care each day to attend to relaxing, letting go, quieting, being still. Let the body relax, give it exercise and rest; let the desires relax, let the insistence on having our own way relax. We don't need to tense ourselves up *for* this or *against* that. We don't have to try to correct, or even to regret, a multitude of faults. Just sit down near Jesus and absorb his peaceful presence. Observe how the peace in him comes from having no personal preference tensions and from having all the dynamisms of his soul well ordered. That's how he can be both peaceful and powerful.

Hear what George Fox, the great Quaker mystic, says: "Be still and cool in thy own mind and spirit from thy own thoughts and then thou wilt feel the principle of God to turn thy mind . . . thou wilt receive his strength and power from whence life comes to allay all tempests, against blusterings and storms. That it is which molds up into patience, into innocency, into soberness, into stillness, into stayedness, into quietness, into God and his power."[3]

THREE

◆

Meditation

*"You shall love the Lord your God with
your whole heart, your whole soul,
your whole mind, and with all your strength."
Mark 12:29*

This is the first and greatest commandment. It is
what the contemplative is trying to do: to come
to this kind of wholeness, totality, integrality, and energy.
The entire heart is to be involved, the entire soul, the entire
mind. Each of these is to be so integrated within itself that
it acts as one. And each of them is to be directed to one sole
focal point, so that they will be integrated with one another.
And all this is to be done with a total commitment of our
energy, with great vigor and ardor. According to Jesus, engaging in this kind of love toward God is the greatest thing
we can do. It is the fundamental thing, the necessary thing,
the first thing and the ultimate thing.

What was said above about stillness is part of this process
of integration, of becoming whole, so that we can love God
with a whole heart, a whole soul, and a whole mind. I spoke
of stillness and pacification of the body through relaxation,
hygiene, and silence, through stillness of the desires of the
senses and of the personality. It is important to see that it is
precisely this letting go—this *relaxation*—of misplaced ten-

sions and stresses in our life that also releases the energy, the *vigor,* with which we may devote ourselves to concentrated, full expression of our love of God.

Spiritual trainers in more than one tradition have likened spiritual life to athletic or artistic performance. The likeness lies in this quality of integral activity, the relaxed, natural, unified, vigorous, or ardent—full powered—act. If either the athlete or the artist is too tight or too self-conscious or too distracted by the desire to do well, the performance will be impeded. Is not a certain type of relaxation the secret of full power in the golf swing or the singing voice? How often a trainer says, Now just let go and give it everything you've got!

The extraneous tensions have to be relaxed, abandoned, renounced, forsaken, so that "everything we've got" can be directed to the one vital value. All the faculties of the human being in turn—body, emotions, sense desires, personality desires, and so on—are to be purified and pacified. Until there is a certain quietness of the usual jangling and jostling of conflicting stresses in these areas, we cannot be integrated, because we will be scattered, and we will, as we've all observed, *feel* scattered, distracted, fragmented. But by relaxation and quiet attention, by faith and devotion, we can be called back into unity. Now I want to carry this same program further by discussing the importance of quieting the restless activity of the imagination and the mind.

The Power of the Imagination

The imagination is a very important part of us. I don't know whether it quite gets its full due from us, whether we take it seriously enough. You may be aware that Emil Coué (of "Every day in every way I'm getting better and better" fame) said that whenever there is a conflict between the will and the imagination, the imagination always wins. "It is," he said, "an absolute rule that admits of no exceptions. We only cease to be puppets when we have learned to guide our imagination. Every one of our thoughts, good or bad, becomes concrete, materializes and becomes, in short, a reality."[1] You may try by sheer willpower to do something or resist something, but if you cannot convert the imagination to the desired position, you will probably not attain what you have willed.

The power of the imagination is shown in psychosomatic phenomena—both sickening and healing. Perhaps you have read reports, usually emanating from faraway places, such as the Phillippines or Africa, of people brought into hospitals, obviously dying, but with nothing wrong with them. Eventually it comes out that someone has cursed them or put a hex on them. They have believed in the power of this and their imaginations have done the rest. Medical science has usually been unable to counter the strength of the imagination, and these people have died. Some daring practitioners have fought fire with fire and got the people unhexed. As soon as their imaginations were convinced that the curse was lifted, they promptly got well.[2]

These are extreme cases. The placebo effect, however, is fairly common and is now well known, both as a medical phenomenon and as a social phenomenon. It works in the classroom and the workplace as well as in the clinic. If the patient and the physician believe (i.e., *imagine*) that the therapy will help, then it probably will, even if there is no active ingredient in it that should in itself cause the healing. If a teacher believes, expects, *imagines,* that certain students are bright or that they are dull, the students will tend to perform in accordance with that expectation. Social classes, in general, who are looked down on by others will find it difficult to arouse in themselves the confidence that liberates their talent and competence.

All this is simply to say that the imagination is powerful, and therefore it is important. We *live* out of our imaginations. We may think or wish that we lived out of our intellect and will, but actually the *proximate* cause of our behavior is the imagination. It is what lies next to our contact with the external or public world. Therefore it is important for us to cultivate the imagination, to take care of it, to feed it properly, protect it, discipline it, train it.

Most of us have always let our imaginations simply run wild. They have grown up without anyone ever giving them any serious attention. The intellect has been trained with scholarship and the will with morality. The feelings have learned to flow in the channels of our culture through socialization. The artistic imagination may have gotten some exercise and direction, but the everyday imagination, what of that? The images that fill our consciousness in our waking and dreaming hours, that govern our world view, our biases and our emphases, our expectations of other people, our interpretations of our experience, and that tyrant of recent years, the self-image.

We need to become aware of the role of our imagination in our everyday inner life. We should spend some time just watching it until we learn what sorts of things it does, and understand how it is connected to our speech, body language, and behavior. We should observe what kind of reveries and fantasies we revolve in our minds when they are free-wheeling. These will accumulate and build on their predecessors until they have constructed a whole world, which for our undiscriminating subconscious mind is indistinguishable from reality.

Thus we can interpret someone's accidental sharp tone of voice as an unfriendly reaction to ourselves, begin to give that person life in our imagination as someone who doesn't like us, therefore be on the lookout for subsequent evidence of hostility, be ready to interpret everything that happens in that light, and of course ourselves show distrust and unfriendliness in turn, which naturally have their effect on the other person; and so by building this thing up in our imagination we can develop a whole atmosphere and relationship of hostility that may be completely false and unnecessary because it all began from something quite accidental. Similarly, by persisting in thinking well of persons, looking for good traits in them, imagining them as pleasant and agreeable, well-disposed toward ourselves, we will enable ourselves to behave in a naturally friendly way to them and elicit friendly responses.

A large area of concern for the cultivation of the imagination is the area of entertainment. What kind of images do we allow entrance to our minds when we go in search of amusement? What kind of books do we read and movies and television watch? What kind of music do we listen to? What kind of dances do we see and do? What kind of sports? What effect do these things have on our spiritual life? It is a large subject and deserving of careful study, but one thing I can tell you: the answer is not "no effect." Everything that ever enters the consciousness has some effect on it and takes up some kind of residence there. Furthermore, there are no thought-tight or feeling-tight compartments in consciousness. Everything seeps into everything else.

Finally, all our problems with poor self-image and unhappiness over our lives are rooted in the imagination. We like to attribute our depressed feelings to circumstances—and indeed there are circumstances under which some people have to live that are enough to depress anyone—but we also know that people can make themselves unhappy in quite neutral circumstances, and on the other hand can rise above an unfavorable quality of life and be happy.

A story I like is that about the gathering in the elevator at nine o'clock on a Monday morning. Here come the business people, the executives and their clerical staff, with their Monday morning blues, looking glum and grumpy. The elevator operator, however, is bouncy and full of good cheer. He greets everyone with a wide grin and a hearty "*Good* mornin'! What a *fine* day!" Finally someone can't stand all this cheerfulness so early in the morning and asks, "What are you so happy about? What's so great about *this* day?" To which the operator replies with enthusiasm, "I ain't never lived *this* day before!"

That's what the imagination can do for you. So it behooves us to guard our imaginations, to train them, to encourage them to feed on inspiring and hopeful fare. In the Epistle to the Philippians we read: "Whatever is true, whatever is honorable, whatever is just, whatever is pure, whatever is lovely, whatever is gracious, if there is any excellence, if there is anything worthy of praise, think about these things" (Philippians 4:8).

That's part of our prayer life. That's a very important part of our contemplative life: the kind of idle ramblings that go on in our minds in the odd corners of the day. If all our psychic faculties, our heart, our soul, our mind, are to be brought to wholeness, so that they can be devoted to love of God, cultivation of the imagination is absolutely necessary.

Our conscious attention wanders about looking for a resting place, a dwelling place, a developing place. We need to prepare a place for it. This is the work of meditation. Meditation is a way of training the attention to adhere to those images and those thoughts which the intellect and will elect to set before it. This is the way we "sit down near" Jesus and stay there without fidgeting long enough to absorb his rhythm.

When people begin to meditate, they sometimes think that it is a kind of self-hypnosis, that because they are exercising the imagination, they are dealing with something unreal. Nothing could be further from the truth. The imagination is in play because we are making things vivid and realistic to ourselves, recreating them interiorly with the richness they could present to our senses externally. But these things recreated by the imagination are not themselves *imaginary,* that is, untrue. Even mythic materials, as we will see in the next chapter, are *true* and do not deceive us.

But the main point about the use of the imagination in meditation is that the faculty itself is being trained. Our attention and our various psychic energies—images, feelings, affections, ideas, intentions, insights, realization—are always in motion, and need to be focused. In meditation we provide a focus and entice them to adhere to it. We try to make this focus more interesting, more appealing, more attractive, than any of its competitors for our attention. This is why the care of the body and the desires needed to be looked to first, because they are our initial distractions when we try to bring ourselves into wholeness and focus on the "one thing necessary." So these disciplines of training the body and the desires must work together with the practice of meditation.

Meditation Must Be Practiced

Although we have some natural talent for it and will sponta-neously fall into it from time to time, if meditation is to be cultivated and brought to the full flower of its potentiality, it must be trained. Considerable discipline and adherence are required. The beginner is usually surprised to discover that what sounds like a simple exercise is rather difficult in execu-tion. And even seasoned practitioners find much to discuss in exchanging notes on problems in their practice. Many of these difficulties can be mitigated by choosing a method that is suited to the mentality and taste of the individual, by finding fresh interest in one's practice through observing one's increasing skill, concentration, and sensitivity to detail, and by exercising the will in patience and perseverance.

However, the American appetite for instant fulfilment will not be gratified. Shopping around for a "crash-course," a marathon workshop that will produce enlightenment in seven extraordinary days, or something of that sort, will not nurture a genuine contemplative. The relaxation of our compulsive demand for success applies very much to our spiritual exercises themselves. There will be many ups and downs and we must be prepared to take them in stride, learning from both, and always going straight ahead.

The best way to practice meditation is every day, at least once, better twice. Discursive meditations, in which there is dramatic visualization, with reflection and thinking about the significance of the subject matter, can go on for an hour. Nondiscursive meditations, in which there is no chain of reasoning, but the mind holds steadily on a single focus while the affections and the will pour out their energy toward it, can be practiced for a quarter to half an hour. It is often a good plan to begin with the discursive meditation and let it pass naturally into the nondiscursive.

There are many methods of prayer and meditation, and most readers no doubt are familiar with a number of these. However, I would like to offer one that seems to me to combine the good features of several methods. Anyone can easily begin it and it can go on to whatever heights divine grace opens to it.

You begin with a gospel scene in which Jesus interacts with someone. For instance, take the story of Bartimaeus, beginning at Mark 10:46.

> And they came to Jericho; and as he was leaving Jericho with his disciples and a great multitude, Bartimaeus, a blind beggar, the son of Timaeus, was sitting by the roadside. And when he heard that it was Jesus of Nazareth, he began to cry out and say, "Jesus, Son of David, have mercy on me!" And many rebuked him, telling him to be silent; but he cried out all the more, "Son of David, have mercy on me!" And Jesus stopped and said, "Call him." And they called the blind man, saying to him, "Take heart; rise, he is calling you." And throwing off his mantle he sprang up and came to Jesus. And Jesus

said to him, "What do you want me to do for you?"
And the blind man said to him, "Rabbi, let me see!"
And Jesus said to him, "Go your way; your faith has
made you whole." And immediately he received his sight
and followed him on the way.

The first thing is to imagine the scene vividly so that the
reality of the event is appreciated. Play it out in imagination
as if you were watching a movie. Then go through the whole
scene again, this time entering into the role of Bartimaeus.
Take time to do this very slowly, filling in the background
and developing the analogy in such a way as to realize that
you yourself are spiritually blind and desirous of seeing.
How *long* you have been blind, how *much* you have missed,
how *eager* you are to see. It is the one thing in life that you
desire. You have heard of Jesus and the wonderful things he
can do. You are convinced that he can enable you to see.
Work on this in terms of your own actual life and selfhood
until the desire and the conviction become single, clear,
strong, and unshakeable. Determine that if ever you have
the chance, you will beg Jesus to give you sight and will not
give up begging until you see.

Your life now becomes a matter of believing that if only
you could get to Jesus, you would see; your whole life is
waiting for him. At last one day he comes. Now there is no
hesitation; this is what you have waited for and prepared
for. Every energy in you centers in one cry, "Jesus, Son of
David, have mercy on me!" At once there are distractions
on all sides, all sorts of voices telling you not to do this. It
seems that everything and everyone is impeding you and
discouraging you. You do not give up but redouble your
efforts.

And then a marvelous things happens. Jesus sends for you.
Dropping your cloak, the last of your pretensions, you run
to him. Everything is in sharp focus now. You cannot hear

the distractions, you are unaware of any discouragement, barrier, impediment, doubt. The whole field of your consciousness is filled by the presence of Jesus turning his full attention on you.

Really feel this. Feel the full force of Jesus' attention turned on you. You have never met a power of conscious attention like this in any other person. Here is personal presence with fullness. When Jesus gives you his attention, the full power of his personal being is turned on you. *He* isn't distracted, *he* isn't scattered, *he* isn't halfhearted, *he* isn't superficial or casual. The full depth and force of his being are attentive to you. *He* is regarding *you* with *his* whole heart, *his* whole soul, *his* whole mind, and with all *his* strength. Stay there and appreciate that.

"What do you want me to do for you?" he asks. There is the central question: the whole meaning of our life boiled down to one simple question. Are we ready to answer it? Have all our desires coalesced into one great desire, one that is worthy to answer that question when it comes? Here the prayer can turn into nondiscursive meditation, repeating this question and hearing it more deeply each time. We comprehend more and more thoroughly that he really is asking it, with the implication that he will do what we ask, and we reach into the depths of our being for the answer.

As we answer, everything in us concentrates to this single intent, as though our whole being had become a single sharp point. We ourselves are integrated in our attention, answering the fully integrated attention that Jesus directs to us. Our one overwhelming desire speaks.

By this time the prayer has reached a high degree of concentration of thought and energy; we are completely absorbed in it. At the point where we experience Jesus giving us his full attention and ourselves concentrating all the meaning and desire of our life into full attention to him, we pass out of moving time into a kind of enduring present moment and linger in that moment as long as we like, without moving. The imagination holds steadily on the realization of Jesus' personal being turned toward us, and we ourselves are responding with a whole mind that has no other thought than what we are answering to him. Our attentions, his and our own, are *locked together*, each pouring itself fully and strongly into the other.

What happens beyond this point cannot be spoken: the actual experience of receiving sight, comprehending how faith has led to this breakthrough and wholeness, and the entrance into a new life, leaving everything behind to follow Jesus.

I think this kind of prayer is good because one has less trouble with distractions in it and it actually brings one right into the presence of God and into a personal relation and interaction. The person of Jesus is so attractive and the dramatic situation of calling forth our own deepest concerns is so absorbing that the ordinary distractions one often has to fight in other kinds of meditation cannot present much competition. Also, all our faculties are involved here: mental clarity to size up our lives and fasten on the one thing we do want; the activity of the will in determining to ask for it; the stimulation of faith and conviction and expectation; the liberation of all the affections and emotions when we are brought face to face with Jesus. Everything comes together and comes to its peak.

The afterglow of this kind of meditation, made first thing in the morning, will last throughout the day and support all the other contemplative practices: the guarding of the imagination, the relaxation of egocentric desires and suspicions; attention and energy applied to our work; compassion and good humor in our interactions with other people. We may want to save a few minutes around the middle of the day to recover some of the feelings of the meditation and give ourselves a boost for the rest of the day. The same contemplation can be repeated in the evening. Or, we might prefer to do a particular meditation for the first time in the evening and then repeat it the following morning.

Meditation is a highly individual affair. One has to experiment a good deal and find something that is real and productive, actually integrating and energizing. Meditation is not a duty to be performed; it is not just a learning device whereby we get ideas; it is not a soothing routine whereby we put ourselves into an altered state of consciousness, or a way of eliciting material from the subconscious so that we can know our empirical personality better. Meditation is a way of meeting God. It is not a matter of thinking about someone who is absent. It is engaging someone who is present, indeed supremely present. It is the realization of this *presence* that is the main point of meditation. The various devices for getting meditation started are all just ways of organizing our total consciousness, our whole mind and heart and soul, and making them hold still and pay attention, without being drawn away by other concerns, long enough to open themselves to the immense reality of the presence of God. Experiencing the presence and reality of God is what it is all about. Anything that can bring you into that is good meditation.

FOUR

◆

The Finite and the Infinite

The traditions of the world that are strong in what we call the contemplative life—a life that leads up to and out from the realization of mystical union with the One and the All—these traditions are also rich in myth and in metaphysics. It is an interesting thing that these three go together: myth, metaphysics, and mysticism. What do they have in common? The union of the finite and the infinite, of the defined and the indefinable.

Myth is a symbolic but concrete presentation of the union of the finite and the Infinite. Usually a story, it may also appear as a ceremony or icon, as building, costume, or dance—or even as landscape. Both concealing and revealing, it is immediately available to the imagination. *Metaphysics* explains theories about the union of finite and Infinite by using concepts and arguments, or by providing phenomenological descriptions followed by reasoning that leads to ontological insight. Many philosophical traditions in both East and West believe that the crucial insight into the basic relation has to come of itself and cannot be captured in concepts and exhaustively explained, although the way to such insight can be prepared. *Mysticism* then grasps the reality directly as a lived experience, without any mediating story or explanation.

All three have to do with the great basic fact of being, that being is both Infinite—transcendent of all form and therefore inconceivable and unspeakable—and possessed of a multitude of expressive, intelligible, often beautiful, sometimes conflicting, processive forms. I will say something about each of these, myth, metaphysics, and mysticism, but especially about metaphysics, for we are now at the stage at which we must work on the fundamental ideas that underlie this whole approach to the contemplative life.

Myth

The Hindus say we should first listen, then we should think, and then we should realize. Receiving the myths is listening; doing metaphysics is thinking; living as mystics is realizing.

Receiving and assimilating myth—whether stylized traditional myths or the mythic dimensions of our own lives—is itself an unconscious experience of the union of the finite and the Infinite. For the mythic embodies the presence of the Infinite, the undefined, the unspeakable, in the artistic guise of the finite, the defined, the variously spoken.

The reality that the myth means to present to us cannot be captured and pinned down and interpreted as a single fixed meaning. The myth seems to be rich with endless particular interpretations. We discover that some people take it one way, others another. We ourselves at various periods of our life, or from different points of view, give a myth different meanings. Yet it remains a singly glimpsed reality, a unitary window on the Great Ultimate.

We receive the myth in its unity, in its simplicity, and yet it reverberates in us in its multidimensional interpretations. We respond to it on several levels at once, and through it to the unspoken Reality it expresses. By the mediation of the mythic image we begin to have lived-experience of being in touch with both the undefined and the definite, although we do not yet know that that is what we are doing. But the exercise of the mythic consciousness is itself a great preparation for the mystical experience that will come later, because it liberates the mind from the literal, one-dimensional, fixed, denotative interpretative habits it often otherwise has, especially in our culture.

In our culture you can find people who have no capacity for mythic understanding. You present them with a story of the miraculous which is luminous with eternal truth—such as the Virgin Birth of Jesus, or Arjuna's vision of the cosmic form of Krishna—and they will ask whether the event portrayed "really happened." They miss the level on which reality and truth are available in the story. Or else they will ask a political question: Is this a story that belongs to *our* religious tradition? If so, it can be true; if not, it is "just a myth." Since some of the stories, especially miraculous birth stories, are very similar, this becomes a crucial question. Again, an opportunity to catch a glimpse of truth and reality has been put aside.

The same truth can be disclosed by many different stories, with different backgrounds and different characters. The fact that the characters are different and the cultural milieu is different doesn't keep the truth from being *true*. The meaning of other people's myths may be just as true as the meaning of our own. But that can be appreciated only after it is understood that the important dimension of the myth is not its historical truthfulness. Even if it did "really happen," that is not the important point for the mythic value. Contemplatives who hope to be nourished by the mythic resources of their own and other traditions must learn to look beyond the question of what happened to the question of what the story means and especially how it sets before us the great mystery of the intersection of the finite and the Infinite.

Take, for instance, the infancy narratives of the gospel. The fathers of the early Christian church had no qualms about handling them, as well as other scripture passages, in an allegorical sense. And today many outstanding scripture scholars of the mainline churches are quite willing to admit that the infancy stories are not to be taken as historical accounts. However, what those stories tell us is something that is profoundly true. Whether or not the angels sang at the birth of Jesus, they certainly should have. Whether the infant was paid homage by shepherds and kings, the poor and humble, rich and learned, of earth in addition to the denizens of heaven, what the gospel writer is saying in a richly imaginative way is what Paul said in a more direct and metaphysical way, "In him all things hold together." Or, if you prefer, here God becomes available to all. That's the beauty of myth: it can mean a great many things simultaneously.

The multiple truths embodied in sacred myth are the first thing the contemplative needs to learn to see. The second thing is that the myth is not really about somebody else. It is about us. Usually the protagonists of mythic stories are drawn on a quite heroic scale. Their characters, personalities, actions, and sufferings are all far above us. Our initial reaction is to think that the heroes and heroines are utterly different from us and that we could never be like that. The next thought is that we are not expected to be. And the one after that is that we can't possibly be and that it is impious to suggest that it is possible. The hero is unique, unparalleled, by definition.

Now, if that were really so, the myth would become dysfunctional. It would not reveal anything important or useful to us. We would be overwhelmed by the marvel, but after that there would be nothing more we could do. Perhaps a tangential function could be invented: if we believe the myth literally, with all its miracles and impossibilities, then our welfare will be somehow assured. But that again is to miss the true meaning and the spiritual power of the myth; it is to refuse to let the myth work in our lives.

To receive the spiritual power of the myth, we have to understand that what it is ultimately doing is revealing the deep truth about ourselves. The stories are about us. It is to us that the angel of the Annunciation proclaims that through the power of the Holy Spirit we will bring forth from our emptiness divine life. Or, taking it another way, nothing has to come into us from outside; the secret of divine life is already within us and needs only to be accepted and nurtured.

It is to us that the baptismal voice is addressed, saying, "You are my beloved child with whom I am well pleased." And if we really *hear* that, we will be driven into a wilderness wherein we will struggle with the question of what that means and what its implications are. And eventually we will find, as was foreshadowed at our birth, that we are lying in the manger as food for the world.

These, and many, many other things are revealed to the contemplative by the great myths of all traditions when we learn to read them at the true level and apply them to ourselves. And we not only apply the traditional myths to ourselves, but ourselves generate myth. Our lives, like the lives of the heroes and heroines in the stories, are mythic if we attend and read them sensitively. Yes, these things "really happened" to us; we really did these deeds. But what is their deep meaning? That is where we find what we call "the meaning of life." When we see this in our own lives, we can understand that there is no conflict between something having "really happened" historically and the much greater importance of its universal and eternal significance.

Furthermore, the mythic values of other people's lives are available to us, just as are those of the larger-than-life figures in our traditional stories. And the mythic values of our lives are available to all other people. This is part of the grand intercommunication, or sharing of life, that we will touch on later as "the communion of the saints." Here it enables us to see another important facet of the union of the finite and the Infinite. We, in our own life, are limited by our particular descriptions and by those events and experiences that characterize our personal histories. But on the mythic level the meaningfulness of everyone's life is offered to us to understand and appreciate as our own. This provides a certain kind of access to the unbounded.

We learn to enlarge ourselves, to live in the unbounded as well as in our particular boundedness, first through the heroic figures of our traditional myths. We see those events and values as characterizing the persons portrayed. If we understand them to have been historical personages, this makes everything more real to us and makes us feel closer to the persons in the story. On the other hand, if we understand them to be ahistorical, then the next step in our learning process is easier: we realize that the story is for us and about us, and we appropriate the meaning of it to ourselves.

Having learned to do this with the shared myths of our culture, we are now prepared to do it with the myths of everyday life, the events in our own life and in the lives of those around us. In this way the full meaningfulness of personal existence becomes available to us, and in the mythic sense we live all lives at once. We discover ourselves in the world of universal and eternal meanings, as well as in the world of particular and temporal events.

Universal and eternal significance—that is the point, that is what makes a story or a historical event mythic. That is why a myth reveals to us the union of the finite, the particular persons and deeds of the story, and the Infinite, the eternal truth manifested there.

But aside from interpreting the particular in function of the universal, the myth may also represent directly the union of the finite and the Infinite. The many stories in various cultures recounting the conception and birth of a divine child in the midst of humanity present mythically to our consciousness the union of the Ultimate Unspeakable and the finite and local particular. Sometimes we are presented, not with a story but with a single image, such as the Virgin Mother who, while remaining One, brings forth Many. Or there is Shiva Nataraja, the dancing God, whose dance is the world in all its manifestations. Such, too, is the crucifix, infinite love in the human gesture of total self-donation. These are mythic expressions and mythic experiences for us. Our consciousness receives them without analysis; they speak to us in a deep and unitary way, despite the fact that they themselves are finite, particular, and composed of parts.

What the myths say *about* the finite and the Infinite, more or less explicitly, is that the Infinite comes first and its expression in the finite follows. We are used to thinking that the real thing, the basic thing, the primary thing, is whether something actually took place in historical time. Then, built on that "fact," we may spin epiphenomena of meanings and significances and interpretations, and bring out morals, elaborate analogies, and make applications. But those we consider to be secondary.

What the myths say implicitly is that Meaning comes first and Expression comes afterwards. The spiritual significance is the primary reality, and the historical event—if any—is secondary, and is only a shadow of the truth. Eternity is not built on time but time on eternity. The question is not, Did that event happen in the past? but, Is that meaning always happening, is it eternally true?

Thus the particular historical event is a kind of sacrament of the eternal truth. We may notice that the sacraments and other symbolic practices as we have them in the various spiritual traditions are that kind of thing: they represent and make present in the particular something that is *always* happening. We celebrate these revelations as events that are rare, special, and separated from profane experience. And that is necessary in the beginning to call our attention to the tremendous power of the meaning. But as we come to see that meaning, we see that it is something that is eternally or constantly going on. The whole of history is a sacrament of the Eternal.

It is the Eternal, the Infinite, that is primary and history, the finite and temporal, that is secondary. The temporal is an incarnation of the Eternal, the embodiment of a transcendent Word. The Word is not about things, as we usually experience words to be, but things are about the Word. We think we have things and we may or may not have words about them. The contemplative knows we have the Word and we may or may not have things about it. It may or may not be incarnated in history but its truth does not depend on that. The meaning, which is the heart of myth, comes first. "In the beginning was the Word" (John 1:1).

This is a delicate point, one that should not be passed over too easily. Understanding it is part of the whole process of resituating the center of gravity of our consciousness, our sense of where we centrally are, from where we look out. The contemplatives teach their pupils that at the center of our consciousness we contact the Infinite, and the goal of our spiritual practices is to experience ourselves as situated there, at the center, in touch with the Infinite, looking out on, in, or through the finite. This is why we strive to readjust our perspective from thinking that finites are the primary real and that meanings, for instance, are secondary, to seeing that the Infinite is the primary and the finite is secondary. Even after you say that you agree, it is easy to fall back into thinking and feeling and behaving as if your world is inverted. We have constantly to remind ourselves that it is the Word that is made flesh and not flesh that is made Word. That was the first lesson of myth.

The second lesson was that the myth is about us and it follows readily from what was just said about the goal of our spiritual life being to bring ourselves into realized union with the Infinite. Since any single event in history is an expression in time of the Eternal Word, all events in time are expressions of the Word, including ourselves. We are Word in expression: primarily meaning, secondarily thing or event in time. The Infinite holds the primacy in us, too. In ourselves we must realize how the Infinite expresses itself, incarnates itself, in the finite. We are used to thinking of ourselves as finites, aspiring to the Infinite. But suppose we experienced ourselves as situated in the central Infinite, and then expressing as finites? Would this not be the profound *metanoia*, the complete reversal and turning around in our most basic consciousness to which in fact we aspire? That is what I think the myths are intended to help us realize.

Metaphysics and Mysticism

When we come to metaphysics, where, by means of *thinking*, we seek to win an understanding that culminates in unitary insight, we already have behind us through our contact with myth some initial personal experience of how the finite and the Infinite are united in our lives. Now we want to see deeper and discover that we as beings are so much more than we had thought we were, so much freer than we had expected, so much closer to one another than we had dreamed possible, because in us, as in all the rest, the finite and the Infinite coexist.

Our usual perception of the world shows us all beings as carefully defined, with distinct edges, all outside one another. It's easy to tell where one individual leaves off and another begins, whether a deed was done by this one or that one. In this view, the beings of the world are all static things, with boundaries and with fixed natures of prescribed limitations. We are finite, contingent, and conditioned beings, and nothing more.

But the metaphysics discovered by the contemplative is rather different. This may be one reason why the mystics who (as if by accident) appear in dogmatic and legalistic cultures nearly always manage to get into trouble with their respective establishments. The heart of the mystic discovery is that we are all one, and that One is unconditioned, unlimited, and undefined. This, of course, is the foundation of neighbor love. Once we get this realization deep into our psyches, we won't have all the usual trouble in loving our neighbors. But until we begin to see *ourselves* in *our* undefined reality, we won't have the freedom, the power, and the energy to love our neighbor in the *neighbor*'s undefined reality.

With respect to all the dualities and dichotomies into which we had usefully divided the world of our experience, a mystic metaphysics refuses to take sides. Nobody denies that dividing, as a vehicle for better understanding, is useful. But along comes the mystic and puts the separated things together, and all the rational people cry Paradox! or worse, Heresy! From the mystic's point of view, however, there is no paradox, nothing bewildering or mysterious.

The mystic sees very clearly on the basis of experience how the unity is there. The mystic claims that both elements of the paradox are simultaneously the case. The bush burns, and yet it is not consumed. Reality is both changing and unchanging. The myth reflects what happens historically, what happens in my life, and what is eternally so. Subject and object are merged in a single consciousness. One is both oneself *and* intimately united with all others. What one does is done by both oneself *and* the Supreme Being. You don't have to choose between them. People sometimes say: I didn't do that, God did it. But when one goes a little deeper, one finds that the action is both one's own and God's, a single act born of confluent energies.

So it no longer makes sense to say, as Philip said to Jesus at the Last Supper: "Yes, I do see you, but I want to see God, the Source and Origin of all." For Jesus in substance replies: "Whoever sees anything at all is looking into the eyes of the Only One Who Is." The Creator is fully present in the creature, because the creature *is* God's act of creating, not some product left over after the act of creation is finished. And the act of creating *is* the active presence of the Creator.

That is why the image of Shiva Nataraja is so compelling. It's very different from the potter and the pot. The potter makes the pot, then gets up and goes about his business while the pot still sits there totally divorced from its maker (though bearing, of course, the mark of its maker's hand). But where the dance is concerned, you have the dance only as long as the dancer is dancing; the dance *is* the dancer *in the act of* dancing. The dancer transcends any particular dance or gesture, but all that the gesture is, is the dancer dancing. The dancer is thoroughly present in the gesture and the gesture cannot be separated from the dancer's act. The image of Shiva as King of the Dance says that God dances and the dancing is the world.

And yet, applying the images to ourselves, this does not inhibit the personal reality and freedom of the human person. On the contrary, this presence to us of the Divine Dancer is precisely what establishes that personal reality and freedom. What makes you to be a person is nothing other than the act of God creating you, an act which makes you to be free and to be yourself with all the rich interior plenitude of subjective being. Such things the contemplative and the mystic see plainly, as obvious. It's really all so simple. Once your eye becomes single, everything is flooded with light.

It takes a while, though, to spell this out, and succeeding chapters will be devoted to clarifying it. The basic point to be made here is that we are both finite and infinite, both conditioned and unconditioned, both describable and indescribable, both particular and involved in all. But because we are used to experiencing ourselves only as the conditioned, descriptive, particular being, we need to turn our attention first to understanding how we are also unconditioned, undefined, and intimate to the Whole.

We tend to experience ourselves by thinking *about* ourselves and feeling *about* ourselves. We form self-images, and we are very careful and concerned about protecting these self-images. Our notion of charity or politeness toward other people is often a matter of not injuring their self-images. We even have all sorts of techniques now for the purpose of acquiring better self-images.

The Real Person Beyond the Descriptive Self

We have developed a cult of the descriptive self, our own personal image industry. It is indeed a matter of images— pictures of the reality, but not the reality itself. It is as though we attended fastidiously to polishing a statue of someone while the living person was actually present with us. The living person is not a statue, not an image of any sort. The living person cannot be pinned down in any set of descriptions: someone is a white American male, a Republican, a Catholic, a businessman, married, six feet tall, weighing 180 pounds, IQ 120, earns $60,000 a year, and has a golf handicap of twelve. He is an extroverted perceptive type born under the sign of Taurus and attached to his own opinions. These are all conventional categories that we use as a kind of shorthand for organizing our affairs for particular purposes that we may have chosen: getting acquainted, identifying people, carrying on a conversation while waiting for the bus. But all these descriptions could be otherwise and that person, the real person living inside, would still be there with the same interior sense of "I am, I am here, I am now, I am I."

It is this interior sense of actually existing in this moment as a sheer "I am" that is the real living person. This person is undefined, indescribable, and transcendent of all categories, roles, and descriptions.

Because it is not defined or confined, the real person is not limited by contrast with beings possessing different definitions. It does not identify itself by seeing how it is distinct and different from others. It does not establish itself in being by drawing a line around its being, outside which are all those other beings which it is *not*.

Because it is not defined, the real person cannot be thought *about*. Whenever you think about something, you are attending to an image, a definition, a description. Similarly, your feelings are about and toward a descriptive image, and your feelings are what they are because the image and the description are as they are, relative to you.

Because it is not defined, the real person is not cut off from other beings; it can flow into them and admit them into itself without fear of losing its own identity and reality, since these are not dependent on setting up some kind of contrast relationship which renders one distinct from those others.

Finally, because the real person is not defined, there is nothing which it *is not*. Therefore, while remaining itself and retaining its personal identity, it can be united with all.

It is this freedom from being only some particular description, and therefore having to protect that description, that liberates us and enables us to give attention and love to other persons. We have a great deal of personal energy, but most of it is tied up in psychological self-defense, in nurturing and enhancing one's self-image. If the only existence and being that I think I've got is my descriptive being, I'm going to be strongly protective of it and defend it at all costs, because that aspect of me that can be described and categorized is very fragile. It can be injured by other descriptive beings. So it's very reasonable to be looking out for Number One.

This is why, if we want to be contemplatives and find out the truth, we have to beware of assuming that our identities are tied up in sets of descriptions, beware of supposing that if we lose our beauty, our health, our money, our job, our social role, we are therefore of no account.

Once we see that our deepest self, the real person in us, is not limited to being any one particular image-self but is actually a child of God, one who simply says "I am I, here, now"—once we really grasp that, all need for this elaborate and expensive defense system evaporates. Then we are free to love others, to will abundant being to them, to all. We no longer have to struggle to maintain a favorable balance of trade in our interactions with them in order to keep a good sense of self-feeling. Our sense of feeling good in being ourselves does not come from any kind of contrast or comparison with others. It comes directly and immediately out of our realization of being a creative act of God, simply unique and absolutely precious.

Furthermore, we are liberated from the boxed-in, local, bounded sense of ourselves we had before. We no longer experience ourselves as a being of fixed nature, of static reality. We have more a sense of ourselves as the *process of be-ing*, as an ever-renewed act, a continuous motion of living, which is God's ever-present act of creating us. Looking toward other persons, we sense them also as creative acts of God, being made fresh from moment to moment, not limited to the descriptions of their past qualities or acts.

This momentary quality of human existence is the foundation for forgiveness. You can forgive a person when you realize that the living person is that person poised right on the verge of moving into the next moment. The real person is not what that person did to me a moment ago, let alone five years ago. So my relationship with the other person, if it is going to be a real relationship, has to be a relationship with the living person, not with the dead, not with the dead past, not even with the dead past of half a minute ago.

What did the angel of the Resurrection say to the women who came to Jesus' tomb? "Why are you looking for the

Living One among the dead? He is not here in the tomb of the dead past." And the living ones in your neighbors aren't in the tomb of the dead past, either. If you want to meet them where they really are, you must meet them where they are *now*, just on the verge of the next moment. To "for-give" is to give abundantly; the prefix in the verb is an intensive. And so our attitude to any and all, enemies and adversaries included, should be a clear will that the person have life and have it abundantly.

Thus forgiveness means entering into the lives of the other persons in order that they may be and that they may be abundantly. We unite with them in their present living moment, loving them where they are. If multitudes of persons were to become free in this way, we all would begin to experience a sense of the Whole as an organic reality, as a single Living One, as a Divine Body. We would be the real *Corpus Christi.* Each of us would be a cell in the Divine Body, and we would also be participants in all the processes and relationships among all the other cells of this Body. We would realize that we are each a part, but also somehow the Whole. With the saints, or realized souls, this becomes a vivid and familiar experience, a perspective on life that even seems obvious, though as we describe it here it may appear a mere fanciful idea.

When we can feel ourselves securely to be this free, *undefined* being which is the creative act of God and simultaneously our own act of being ourselves, then we can also express ourselves freely and creatively as *finite* beings. Metaphysical reflection leads to insight, which leads to artistic manifestation. Any artist, filled with the formless realization of great truth and beauty, gives expression to this realization in some particular form of sound or shape or color or action.

We experience ourselves as actively speaking our word, itself an overtone of the Eternal Word. The word arises out of silence, the Void of the Absolute, transcendent of any particular form, but as spoken it takes a form, takes a body, becomes incarnate in a particular place and time and circumstance. And we consciously put our whole selves into this word which we speak by our lives. Thus we realize ourselves as both the formless one, undefined—and in this sense infinite—and one expressed in form, thus finite.

The relation between the two aspects, infinite and finite, is the relation of *incarnation:* without ceasing to be formless in our central reality, we take on expressive form. Isn't that the dogmatic formulation of the Incarnation: "Without ceasing to be God, the Word became man"? That, in my view, epitomizes the basic metaphysics of the contemplative life.

It is easy enough to see, now, how this is the foundation for mystical experience, and an ongoing unitive life. The corresponding mystical realization is a spontaneous perception of all being (i.e., God, ourselves, other persons, the entire cosmos), as divine creative organic process: diversity intensely unified by free acts of self-giving and involvement, transcendent formless being taking on forms of intelligence and beauty, parts of the Whole experiencing themselves as also coexistent and coincident and confluent with the Whole.

The mystic is one who directly experiences union with God or with the Whole. But if the God with whom one is united is a Creator God, then one is united with this great act of creating. If the God with whom one is united is a God who becomes incarnate in our world, then one is united with this act of taking flesh in particularity. If one is united with the Whole, then one extends one's sense of expression and incarnation to the entire process of the divine cosmic life. And this becomes one's basic, natural, spontaneous sense of how things are, where one is situated, from where one looks out to experience whatever one experiences. The whole cosmic movement becomes content of one's interior life.

One experiences one's life, then, in three noncontradictory, nonexclusive ways: (1) as *transcendent* of all particularity (i.e., not dependent on, or limited to, or exhausted by, any particular form or description); (2) as incarnate in *particularity,* especially as freely and artistically chosen and expressed; and (3) as *cosmic,* as so deeply involved with all other beings as to form with them one continuous organic process.[1] And all these are the Divine Life, the life of union with God. Reality is both infinite and finite, and in this divine union we realize our true identity by experiencing our participation in both the Infinite and the finite.

As contemplative practice leading into this experience of divine union, we can practice *listening* to the *myths* of tradition and of daily life, *thinking* through the *metaphysics* that clarifies our relation to the whole Reality, and *opening ourselves* to the spontaneous appreciation of this truth, the *mystical realization* of living in this unitive state.

FIVE

♦

Sin and Salvation

The contemplative is not a dweller in an ivory tower, cut off from the world, oblivious of the suffering of humanity. On the contrary, the contemplative is one who is devoted to seeking the way out of evil and suffering. If we can understand the roots of our distress and the secret of our release, then we can act in the world to alleviate the pain.

There is a great deal of evil in the world. Some of it is petty and annoying. Some of it is unbelievably horrible. And some of it is institutionalized among us, praised, honored, and supported to such an extent that many of us cannot even recognize that it *is* evil.

The "Mystery" of Evil

It is not, in my view, sufficient to cry Mystery! in the face of evil. This gives expression to our feelings of bafflement and frustration, but it doesn't help much beyond alerting us to the fact that the problem is deep-seated and that if we want to try to do anything about it, we must go very deeply into ourselves. We can't expect to succeed if we merely shift things around a bit politically, make and enforce some laws, punish offenders, deter those who might injure us, and preach morality to the millions. None of these methods has made it possible for human beings to give up doing evil.

There is a story about an ancient Greek legislator who stood up to address a meeting of the city fathers. The assembly was debating the passing of a resolution concerned with punishing a vassal city-state that had failed to pay tribute. The issue was whether they should send the army out and kill them all. When our man took the floor, he said: "For thousands of years people have been trying to find ways of preventing crime. What do they do? They keep increasing the severity of the punishment on the supposition that this will deter the criminal. But it doesn't work. You've got to find out what is causing the criminal to act. One thing I know. As long as people are poor, hungry, and oppressed, they will continue to do what they feel they have to do to stay alive, and all your threatened punishments are not going to deter them."

Punishment and threat of punishment—even eternal punishment—are not an adequate response to evil. And neither, in my view, is meditation on the mystery of evil, how strange it is, why God tolerates it, how incomprehensible it is, how it is an ineradicable part of our nature, or whatever it is that religious people think of when they meditate on "the mystery of evil." I believe it is part of the contemplative's vocation to trace evil to discoverable roots and find out how to deal with it effectively.

But is the prospect of a world without evil an acceptable prospect? When someone proposes actually getting rid of evil, people either laugh or grow stiff and resistant. They remind you that evil, like the poor, you will always have with you. You can't change human nature. Or, only God can destroy evil, and he will do it only in his own time. The message is, don't try to remove evil, just punish it.

I have an idea that this darkly stubborn view can be traced to the belief that evil is a kind of fundamental archetype in the furniture of human consciousness, and perhaps in the structure of being. Evil is necessarily there as a foil for good. Take evil away, and everything would be thrown out of balance. Without it, how would we learn to value and have a distinct sense of the good? Without hell, how would the good people who are saved properly appreciate the fate they managed to avoid? How could people be tested to see if they deserved heaven unless they had a chance to do evil? And it wouldn't be a real test unless some of them actually did do evil. How could you sort and classify people unless some were good and some bad? How could there be any stories to tell (or even fun things to do in real life) unless there was big evil to overcome and little evil to do on the sly?

I once polled some people in a study group with the question, "Which world would be better, one that was all good, or one with both good and evil in it?" A surprising number of people thought that a world with evil in it would be better than one without it. Putting aside the contradiction in terms, I asked these good religious people why they preferred a world with evil. One woman summed up what is probably the sense of many when she said that a world in which everyone was good would be "blah." I wonder what she thinks heaven will be like.

Others debated how you could have any growth in such a world. How would you develop character? It reminds me of an old *Peanuts* comic strip sequence. Charlie Brown is asking Lucy why life is so hard and full of adversity. She replies that adversity is good for you because it builds character. Charlie Brown then wants to know what we need character for, to which Lucy answers: to cope with adversity.

Obviously we have some curious emotional attitudes toward evil. We are very interested in it and very attached to it. In fact we build our lives around it to a great extent. Think of the unemployment that would result if everyone were good! There would be no need for police, military personnel, prisons, bill collectors, the FBI, the CIA, law courts, and above all, lawyers. And for that matter, what would the religions do? What would the preachers preach about? As the cannibal said, "If we were to give up eating people, it would upset our whole internal economy!"[1]

Joking aside, it is not helpful when people complain that explaining evil is tantamount to excusing it, as though searching for the social and psychological reasons for crime is espousing some form of determinism and holding that the criminal is not responsible. If we are really interested in getting rid of evil, or at least in diminishing it, surely the first step is to try to understand its causes. It seems to be a more fruitful approach than expending all one's energies in assigning blame for it, or making a theology about it, or simply mourning and marveling over it. What matters is whether we can actually succeed in doing something about it.

One thing should be said at the start: Evil is not simply the opposite, or reciprocal, of good. This is a mistake many people make. Good and evil are not an inseparable pair, like inside and outside, or concave and convex. They are not mutually referring and dependent. Evil cannot stand by itself, cannot originate anything. It can only react to what already exists, to distort or destroy it. Good can stand alone and can create; it can bring something into being out of nothing. The good does not have to be referred to something else, to its contrast with evil, in order to exist or in order to be conceived. Evil does have to be referred to good in order to be conceived, and in order to exist has to react against something good that exists. Evil is dependent on good; good is not dependent on evil. Evil is relative always and cannot be absolute. Good can be relative but also can be absolute. And Absolute Being must be Absolute Good.

Since evil is relative, we cannot sufficiently account for suffering and the misdeeds that cause suffering by saying that the agent is evil. It is the evil in the agent that has to be accounted for. And since evil is always relative, never absolute, then evil *can* be accounted for. It is not ultimately and necessarily inscrutable, even though it may be very subtle and very complex, its roots exceedingly tangled.

It is my contention that evil comes about because of what is perceived as a basic metaphysical need in the agent, the need to stay alive, to maintain one's being. Where moral evil is involved, the agent identifies exhaustively with the image-self, the descriptive self, and instinctively recognizes the primordial need to stay in being. It is the self-image which the agent endeavors to maintain in being and enhance in being, because the agent believes that this is *all* the self-being the agent has, and that if the agent does not tend to its sustenance and welfare, it will suffer diminishment, because nobody else is going to sustain it.

The diminishments can be of various types, from loss of one's bodily life, through loss of one's property or reputation or the ability to earn a living or otherwise act as one wishes, to loss of one's self-esteem and sense of feeling good. It is in order to avoid these life-losses that people do what we call evil. (I am not saying that every act that moves to protect against such losses is evil. I am saying that when there is an evil act, it will be a move to protect against such loss.) In the concrete, we find that evil is not usually done just as a response to the *possibility* of loss. Nearly always the agent of evil is a person who has already *actually* suffered severe losses on some level of life. (Again, I am not saying that everyone who has suffered loss will engage in evil, but that someone who commits evil will probably be found to be someone who has suffered loss.)

The Descriptive Self

Let us analyze this loss in greater detail. We begin with the descriptive self. It is identification with the descriptive self that makes evil acts, or sin, possible. Not inevitable, just possible. The description consists of all those categories and quality or quantity ratings by which we customarily introduce ourselves to others and image ourselves to ourselves: our occupation, our relation to spouse or parent or child, our nationality, our religion, our race, our wealth, our fame, our achievements; perhaps even some special feature that looms large in our social life, such as sexual orientation or some physical or mental handicap, or a drug dependency or a prison record. And how many of us build our lives around the particular description we give in these terms.

This is how we think of ourselves and how we think of other people. Our self-esteem and our sense of having a satisfactory life are framed in these terms. We struggle and strain to be able to say to ourselves and others, I have the description that is valued in this society. Or, if we cannot attain that, then we try to get the description that we do have valued: we declare that being the way *we* are is just as good and beautiful and natural and proper as being the way *they* are. But we still think that we *are* that description. And our life consists of trying to get the description valued or trying to get the valued description. It doesn't occur to us that our value doesn't lie in the description at all.

Another thing that happens when we define ourselves by descriptions and comparison and relations is that the value comes from scarcity and envy. As long as I have the only Mercedes-Benz on my block, I'm an important person. When every garage on the street has a Mercedes in it, it doesn't count anymore. It was the comparison, the contrast, that gave the value and gave me a sense of who I am. Similar things are true of our sense of achievement. If everyone can run the four-minute mile, I have no sense of accomplishment in it. All this seems quite right to us. We even have a wise saying, "Where all are honored, no one is honored." Our notion of value seems to be that in order for it to be valued it has to be scarce. There must be not enough to go around. It's the fact that some people—even most people—*don't* have it that makes it valuable, that makes it good. Deprivation, *nonbeing,* is the foundation of this sense of value.

Our feeling good about ourselves thus depends on other people feeling bad. They must wish that they could have what we have, or do what we do, and *not have it,* in order for our possession or our achievement to be important. If no one else wanted to have it or do it, then even if I were the only one in the world to have it or do it, I would be worthless. Comparison, contrast, someone up, someone down, this is the way our judgment of our life goes.

What happens when we are not top dog in such a comparison? When we have drawn the short straw? When we are deprived, oppressed, rejected, ignored, despised, scorned, ridiculed? We are hurt, not only in our physical poverty or cultural deprivation, but in our sense of ourselves. My "who I am" is injured, and this injury seeks compensation. The injured self feels that it *has to have* compensation in order to *maintain its being.* Its homeostasis somehow has to be restored. It feels the need of being "balanced," or "getting even."

Because the sense of value is a contrast sense, this injury can be compensated *either* by attaining the value of which we were deprived, *or* by doing down someone else, perhaps with respect to some quite different quality, so that in comparison with them we now are on top. But then *that* underdog will in turn have to do the same thing in compensation for *that* injury, and a chain reaction is set up. This is the sin chain whereby the hurts of one generation of interacting persons or races or classes or nations are passed on to succeeding generations.

It doesn't come about simply because people are evil or greedy or weak or proud or self-willed. It comes about because of the way we have structured our sense of value, making it depend on comparison, on contrast, on scarcity, on deficiency, on deprivation, on disappointment, on frustration, on injury. And this in turn comes about because of our assumption that we *are* only our descriptions, our relations to persons and institutions, our possession of a set of definable attributes.

It is important to understand this if we want to work in the area of peace and justice, to lift up the poor and free the oppressed. We must understand that fighting, defeating, depriving, and oppressing are *systematic necessities of our present mentality*. We have to have the contrast in order to have the sense of value, in order to have the sense of who we are, in order to *maintain ourselves in being*.

Two Kinds of Freedom

Let me say something now about the kind and degree of freedom in which the agent of evil operates. Usually this agent is a person who has suffered significant diminishments and injury on some level of body and/or soul, and has become correspondingly suspicious of others. Therefore the agent seeks urgently to protect the self with security, pleasure, and power, and to put down, diminish, dominate, and destroy others. All this is done to keep the self in being, in bigger and better being.

The agent does not have to do this in any particular way, at any particular time. The person exercises choice-freedom on any particular occasion. I make a distinction between *choice-freedom* and *creative freedom*. The stimulus for choice-freedom originates in the environment, which presents me with alternatives: should I order steak or fish, pie or cake? The various foods are there in the outer environment, and my own hunger as part of my inner environment puts pressure on me to make a choice. What is specific about choice-freedom is that both the alternatives among which you may choose and the inner urgency to make such choices come from the environment—where environment includes feelings that are inside yourself. Usually when people think of freedom, they have in mind this kind of ability to make a choice among alternatives.

But there is another kind of freedom, namely, creative freedom. It means that you act from yourself as author, as from a first origin or source. You are not acting in reaction to some kind of external stimulus. You start the action. And when we apply this notion to God and the nature of divine love, we may begin to understand the true nature of creative love. God does not love you or me because we are worthy, desirable, or attractive. God's love is not a reactive love, not a choice-love. God is the author of all that is. Everything starts in and with God whose action and love are never determined or elicited by anything in the environment. Creative love is self-initiated, expansive, and in a word, creative.

So what I am saying about evil acts is that they have to be cases of choice-freedom, not of creative freedom. There is no way that anyone can do evil for its own sake. Evil is done only when there is some kind of a choice situation presented by the environment, whether within or outside the agent. And the agent believes that if one doesn't act to secure and augment one's own life, the job won't get done and one will "die" in some sense or other. One has to try to stay in being, and this need exercises a great pressure. It is behind all particular occasions of evildoing, although any single action can be quite free.

In one's usual consciousness, the agent may "know" that the act is "wrong," at least in the sense that it is disapproved by the agent's community (and what is disapproved, or "wrong," may vary to some extent in different cultures). Unconsciously, though, the agent thoroughly *knows* in the deepest way that what is going on is a "seeking to preserve one's life." Through an intricate and complex series of derivations, that need is what finally issues in the unkind word or the mass murder, and all the sins in between. They are all forms of "seeking to preserve one's life" because one believes the lie that "if I don't seek to preserve it, it won't be preserved." This is the "father of lies," the falsehood on which all sin is based.

I don't believe this is the same as saying that all sins are based on either pride or concupiscence. Both of those seem to me to suggest that one desires something in excess of what one fundamentally needs. Nor do I believe that sin is anything so sophisticated as "preferring oneself to God." That sounds impressive in theory, but I am extremely dubious about finding it in actual cases. Beneath anything that might take such extravagant and pretentious flights, I think there is a quite raw urgency simply to exist—but for a *person,* this will mean existing on levels of self-esteem, value and meaning, as well as elementary security, nourishment, and relief from pain. That is why I think the bottom line is a flaw in knowledge—a belief in a falsehood—rather than a flaw in the will.

Therefore I also think that it is a mistake to imagine that evil is chosen under conditions of maximum freedom. Evil is chosen, it seems to me, under great pressure, the pressure to preserve oneself. Of course this gets elaborated and twisted. One special form of it can be that one chooses to do something defined as "evil" just in order to prove that one is "free" and independent and can go against everyone else. But it is not hard to see the poverty of creative expression that has to resort to such terms in order to gain a sense of its own reality. This contrived "experience of being free" is merely an effort to shore up the insecure self and make it feel that it is real, that it exists. This expresses profound distrust of communion with other people, that is, terrible *fear;* and it is all based on a fundamental falsehood about how being is constructed.

People don't knowingly and willingly choose to believe in falsehood. People do believe the falsehood—that no one cares enough about them to preserve them in being—because they feel so insecure and inadequate. After that, it's very hard to get them to feel secure in communion with other persons and to believe that they are loved. But to imagine that sin originates in pure freedom, I think, is a great mistake.

I propose instead that sin originates in lack of sufficient believable unconditional love. And this lack forms a chain: People who have not experienced being loved adequately aren't able to love adequately, and so their children and other companions are impoverished in turn and pass this deficiency on to all whom they touch, and so on. But it doesn't start in freedom; it starts in created finitude and scarcity on which a contrast value system is built. Then, within that system, choice-freedom operates. But the evil act is never free in the sense that a good act can be free. There is no such thing as creative or absolute freedom to do evil, comparable to the creative, original, freedom to do good.

It is sometimes said that the root of sin is wanting to be God in your own right. There is nothing wrong with wanting to be divine. After all, God wants nothing more than to share the fullness of divine life with us. But it's that "in your own right" that betrays the distrust of any donor of divine life. One who feels this way is convinced that the only way to be safe is to control everything oneself. This isn't *pride*. This is *fear*. Terrible, rock-bottom, existential fear. And just as love casts out fear (1 John 4:18), so fear arises only from belief in lack of love. But this is a falsehood.

Salvation through Love

Now, if this is an accurate analysis of sin, then the way out of sin is to see through the falsehood, to be really convinced that someone else *is* sustaining you, that you don't have to sustain yourself, that you are already given more affirmation, nurturance, respect, love, life, joy than you can even imagine desiring. If you can really *believe* that someone else is sustaining you, then all the self-defense operations which result in sins are going to evaporate, because they are no longer needed.

It is at the moment when you perceive this truth and really accept it, believe yourself to be loved—permit, agree, allow, consent to be loved and sustained by another—it is at this moment that *salvation* takes place. It is when this deep metaphysical need to be loved and sustained is *met and satisfied* that one's life is really saved, preserved, kept from destruction.

"Salvation," therefore, is not a matter of offering sacrifice to appease God. This is a primitive, not to say barbaric, notion. God doesn't need appeasing. God's "attitude," if we may so put it, is one of eternal steadfast love. What needs "appeasing" is the craving for life of the descriptive self and the fear of destruction in the sinner. Salvation is effected by someone loving the sinner and *convincing* the sinner of that love. "Greater love than this no one has, that one should lay down one's life for one's friends" (John 15:13). If the convincing gesture is "dying for you," then that gesture can be used because it convinces the sinner of the love. It is the love and the conviction of being loved that is salvific.

This proposal, obviously, is to be distinguished from the doctrine of vicarious atonement. The latter is based on the idea of substitution, where one person dies in place of another. We had an instance of this during the Second World War. It was a rule in one Nazi concentration camp that if anyone tried to escape, he would be shot; if he succeeded in escaping, ten others would be shot. It didn't matter who. In this case, when the father of a family was picked to be shot, a fellow prisoner, a priest named Maximillian Kolbe, offered to take his place and was, in fact, shot to death. This was substitution. One man died instead of another.

But when we approach the question of eternal salvation, if someone is said to die "for you," it is not the dying qua dying that is salvific, but the dying qua loving. It is true that we must die in order to enter into glory, but that is not a dying that someone else can do for you, any more than someone else can be happy for you. Dying and being happy are things that you yourself must do, and in fact dying and entering into glory are two sides of the same coin. This latter point is central in the New Testament, where Jesus' being "glorified" is spoken of as a synonym for his dying.

What dies, in our case, is the ego image-self. It is clinging to that ego image-self that separates us from the Holy of Holies within us. And when it dies, together with all its works and pomps, when it is rent from top to bottom, then the glory that is in the central sanctuary pours out and floods everything we are and do, and we are truly reconciled with the Living God within us.

But what will enable us to rend that veil that hides us from our true self? How can we get past the need to clutch our life to ourselves and seek to preserve it? That is where "dying for you" as the extreme proof of love is what performs the miracle. It is an ultimate gesture intended to convince. If you are convinced of that love, your curtain disintegrates.

It is in this sense that we are saved by believing in God's love. It is at the moment when we really believe that we already have full life—that we can let go and be sustained by another, by that other's love—that we are saved. If we go on trying to preserve our lives, we lose them. If we give up clutching our descriptive life for the sake of believing that our transcendent self is sustained by God's love of us—that is to say, for the sake of the Good News—then we can possess eternal life (Mark 8:35).

Please notice that (at least in my interpretation) this is not a quid pro quo: if you do this, then I will do that; if you believe, then I will save you. It's just an empirical spiritual fact. That's how things are. If you believe (cling to) falsehood, you lose being. If you accept the truth of love, you win security.

Two other things need to be said about this salvific love: it is directed to the transcendent self, and it is unconditional. The salvific love is not a response to some attractive attribute in the beloved. The entire description of the beloved is irrelevant. The beloved is not loved because of being worthy of the love or eliciting the love in some way. Nor does anything about the description deter or inhibit love. God's salvific love is absolutely impartial because it is absolutely creative; it is not dependent on anything in the beloved's description.

If God's love did depend on one's description, it could not be absolutely secure, for that description can and does change and one would be always fearful of losing God's love and esteem. If the love were contingent, or conditional, it would not be salvific, for it is just its being absolutely secure that enables us to let go our need to protect and augment ourselves.

But God's love is not conditional. We *cannot* do anything to deserve God's love—for which reason it is called grace; and we *need not* do anything to provoke it. It is always already there. Any love that is going to be salvific must be of this type, absolutely unconditional and free.

Now perhaps we can understand why we can't expect a "self" which is conceived and experienced as only a bundle of descriptions to be able to love its enemies, conceived and experienced as their descriptions. That is a contradiction. That is why people don't do it. Only the self that has realized itself as transcendent of any particular descriptions, so that it can afford to lose them, is able to love the enemies of those descriptions, or to love one's enemies in spite of their descriptions.

Before you can tell people to love their enemies, you've got to convince them that they are more than what the enemy attacks or threatens or diminishes. You've got to convince them that they are really children of God, spiritual transcendent beings who can incarnate themselves in any kind of world, in all sorts of descriptions. You've got to convince them that they are loved and sustained, that they are secure, that they are free. Then they will be able to relax their clutching hold on this small self threatened by enemies (including the interior enemies of psychological conflicts) and be able to love in turn. *You can't do it the other way around:* first obliging people to love their enemies and then awarding them something called "salvation" as a prize. That would be conditional love, and if there is anything that is the opposite of salvific, it's conditional love. No, first people must be "saved"; that is, they must be convinced that they are securely, unconditionally loved and sustained, and then they will be *able* to let go their ego-defenses and live the divine life. Loved themselves, they will love others.

It is true, though strange to say, that most people resist being loved. But God is persistent. God is patient and does not give up. God leaves ninety-nine sheep in the fold and goes after the one that is lost *until he finds it and brings it back*. God sweeps the house clean and searches for the lost coin *until she finds it*. People who have been hurt are very distrustful; they cannot easily believe that someone loves them unconditionally. They fear it's a trick, or that things will change, or that it's not really unconditional but actually imposes an enormous obligation of gratitude (we encourage that one, you know, even while claiming that God's love is unconditional), or that somehow there is a diminishment in being a recipient.

All this comes of not understanding the nature of unconditional, creative love, that it is addressed to the true self which transcends all the descriptions. And institutionalized religion hasn't always helped us understand. It has often represented God's love, or even approbation, as highly conditioned. This naturally terrifies people. God has to work a long time to overcome these fears, this distrust. But this willingness on

God's part to wait and to keep trying is the divine mercy, or pity. Nor is death a cut-off, after which it's too late and God has to give up. God never gives up, but pursues people forever, hoping to convince them that they are unconditionally loved. This is *God's* "radical optimism"!

So I believe that if we try to penetrate this mystery and understand what evil is and how it arises, then we will be in a better position to try to do something about it by offering people unconditional love—the only thing that really works. And even it works only if it is believed and accepted. But preaching against sin, meditating on how bad it is, remorse, and punishment—none of these gets at the root of it, the lack of love; on the contrary, they increase the stress, the tension, the sense of danger and injury.

We can move from a sinful life to a life of divine love only after we ourselves have thoroughly accepted God's unconditional love. Preaching and meditation therefore should be directed to *that*. And we should be careful to stress the *un*-conditional. Not: God loves us if we are obedient, or if we believe, or if we join the right church, or if anything, or as anything, or with reference to anything. And we are not to feel guilty over not *fully* accepting God's love. That's a back door way of reintroducing the sense of condition.

So let us contemplate the mystery of the divine love, an original, creative, unconditional love directed to us as our transcendent selves, irrespective of any description we may have or not have. Opening ourselves to this realization and letting it really take hold of us so that we are thoroughly convinced of it, let us feel a great relaxation of tension, of fear, or distrust, as we repose in this sense of absolute security and inpouring eternal life.

◆

SIX

Heart of Jesus, Root of Reality

It was from the nineteenth-century Hindu saint Sri Ramakrishna that I learned to approach the spiritual life from the point of view of conceiving God as both with form and without form. This allows both a dualistic devotion and a nondualistic realization of God as valid. What was special about Sri Ramakrishna was his ability to enter deeply into various religious traditions of the world, ones he found in his own native India and other religious traditions that he knew about. He declared he found them all valid. In particular, he viewed as equally acceptable both the devotional attitude that sees God as one to love and worship, and the mystical experience in which the worshiper is lost in the Divine. Instead of debating the theoretical merits of dualism and nondualism, he claimed to have tested them empirically and found both true.

There has long been quarreling between dualists and nondualists. Eastern spiritual traditions are often hospitable to nondualists; these mystics feel that they and Ultimate Reality, or the Ground of Being, are one. If they speak of "God," they say that in the mystic union it is all but impossible to tell where one's soul leaves off and God begins, so thoroughly interpenetrated is the soul that is taken up into the Divine

Reality. On the other hand, the Abrahamic religions, Judaism, Christianity, and Islam, tend to be very strongly dualistic and to hold that there is a great gulf between the Creator and the creature, one that cannot be crossed, one that will remain a barrier for all eternity, no matter how much grace God gives to the creature. So among Western theologians there is great resistance to any form of nondualism such as we find in some Hindu and Buddhist positions. However, it should be noted that not all Hindus are nondualists. Some are adamant in opposing that position. And the average worshiper, in the East, as in the West, is a practicing dualist.

It strikes me, however, that the two are related. Suppose that you believe in nondualism and are determined to try to have realization of God in a nondualistic way. Right away you run into the obstacle of the ego, which prevents you from having the desired realization. In order to overcome the obstacle of the ego, a very useful practice is to have devotion to God in a dualistic framework. You can have devotion to God as the servant of God, the worshiper of God, the instrument of God. All this tends to erase the ego-self, as one becomes the instrument of God—and we see Jesus doing this too. Eventually there is nothing left of self. No matter what you do or say or think, you attribute it all to the agency of God. Jesus himself said that he did not do anything on his own authority: he spoke only what the Father gave him to speak. This helps one get rid of the ego; when this happens, the nondualistic experience becomes available and you're able to say: "The Father and I are one. . . . What do you mean when you say 'Show us the Father'? He who sees me sees the Father."

Now reverse the situation. Suppose you believe in dualism, so you are going to practice devotion to God in a dualistic framework. That means that you have ardent, impassioned love for God. God is the Beloved. And this love relationship deepens as desire increases. You find that love means that you must ultimately enter into the Beloved's own heart, so that you feel from within everything that transpires there, so that you can look out through the Beloved's own eyes, feel what the Beloved feels, will what the Beloved wills, so that you become thoroughly united with the One whom you love. Thus the very pressure of dualistic love will force you into a nondualistic realization.

Jesus and Nondualism

Jesus wants us to be related to him in a nondualistic way; his whole intention and the whole point of his life is to give himself without reserve to us and into us, so that he may live in us. Is not this the meaning of his prayer:

> "Father, I desire that they also, whom thou hast given me, may be with me where I am, to behold my glory which thou hast given me in thy love for me before the foundation of the world." (John 17:24)

When Jesus as teacher, as disciple-maker, desires that everyone should be like himself—and that is the goal of every sincere teacher—it means that he wants us to experience his freedom, his interior freedom from all of these inhibitions and fears and cravings and clutchings we've been talking about. He wants us to enjoy his self-realization, his union with the Source of Being, whom he calls Father. It's his own interior experience that he wants to share.

This means that the rest of us are to have this kind of experience. Whatever is reported of Jesus, therefore, is to be replicated in us. Just go through the Gospels and find out what he is like. It's a revelation of what is in store for you, what is expected of you, what is promised to you, and what you in your profoundest reality always already are. What he experiences in his consciousness, we are to experience in ours. We are to enter into his very heart, the center of his being. Surely this must be what his thorough self-gift means, what being "with him where he is" means, what hearing everything that he has heard from the Father means, what being engrafted into his life so that his blood flows in our veins means.

Entering into the heart of Jesus means also entering into our own heart, the center of our being, the core of our existence. Can we find this in experience, actually do it? Yes, but everything superficial must be laid aside.

We are coming now to the mystical detachment. We are not talking about the usual abstinences, about the avoidance of unkindness to a neighbor, and so forth. We are now going to get into it much more deeply. There are layers and layers of superficiality. Everything, before you come to the heart itself, is comparatively superficial.

Let us retrace briefly the steps we have taken to arrive here. Saved by our acceptance of God's unconditional love for us, we are freed from the need to insist on our personal pleasure and power. We do not make the attainment of possessions and privileges the chief goal of our life. We do not concentrate on the pursuit of bodily pleasures, stimulations, and comforts. We do not identify with our success or failure in our career. We do not refuse to rejoice in God's life because of disappointments in human relations.

Many of the descriptions of the superficial self have thus been stripped off. But they may have been replaced with some new ones: I belong to such a culture, such a religious tradition; I have such a role or office in my tradition; I follow such a spiritual path. And even if these have been transcended, we are left with our sense of our own personality and with our ideas of how the God-world relation is structured: our psychology and our theology. These are much harder to "unknow," and many people hold that we are not to give up identifying with them at all.

Probably not very many Christians would be willing to do what is reported of a certain Zen adept. He was well known as a master in their tradition. But he had in the vestibule of his home a calligraphy hanging on the wall, a beautiful piece of writing, which read: "I have long since forgotten what is Zen Buddhism." He had followed beyond the pointing finger and had seen the moon.

But what else is the contemplative life for? It is where the great risks can be faced, where folkloric religion can be outgrown and the naked Reality entered into by the naked spirit. In the depths of the contemplative life, there should no longer be any secrets, any euphemisms, any tales told to children, but the way should be clear to find the Real beyond finite descriptions.

One contemporary who pursued passionately this quest for the Real was Dom Henri Le Saux, better known as Swami Abhishiktananda, a French Benedictine who lived in India as a sannyasin, or Hindu monk. He has this to say about entering the heart of Jesus:

> As he passes from depth to depth in his own heart, the awakened disciple reaches the ultimate depth of the Heart of Jesus (. . . a pointer to the ultimate recesses of the source of being). Then, passing beyond all, beyond himself, freed from all bonds, even mental ones, he finally comes to the Source where in his eternal awakening he discovers that *he is*.[1]

This surely is a good description of the realization that Jesus himself had, that he is the Son of God who is Yahweh, I AM. He has traced his being back to the Source, which he calls Father, as a personal name.

In India they have pilgrimages on which the devotees trace the sacred river back to its source in the holy mountains above the world. It's a good analogy for our spiritual life.

Abhishiktananda became acquainted with many such things through his contact with Hindu monks. For instance, he learned much about the deeper meaning of I AM from the great mystic, Sri Ramana Maharshi. Ramana taught his disciples to ask themselves repeatedly, "Who am I?" until their habit of identifying with their predicates and descriptions had worn thin and dissolved, and they could unite purely with the unmodified I AM. Abhishiktananda found that distinct traditions do have certain things in common and that they flow together again, even as they came out of the one source. We are all to find that we are the offspring of the One Who Is, and we find this experientially only when we reduce ourselves to a bare "I am" without any predicates whatsoever.

This is a very austere doctrine, and the teachers of the mystic way have little pity for their pupils when they are engaged in revealing to them adult teaching. But there are some gentler approaches to this point.

The Jesus Path

Jesus, as disciple-maker, calls himself the Way, *hodos,* a road. The road is something you can walk on; it gets you from here to there. Jesus is such a path. The passing from depth to depth on the way into his heart corresponds to a passing from depth to depth in our own heart, where "heart" means the core of our existence, not just the seat of the affections. We can walk on this road which is Jesus first by petitioning him, then by studying him, later by imitating him, and by dialoguing with him. But after we have practiced these disciplines for some time, if we are to enter his heart, we must get into his own consciousness.

At first this will be his consciousness of the world, especially of people, their situations, their suffering. Renouncing our attachment to our own temperamental attitudes, we try to enter into the outlook of Jesus, to see with his eyes and feel with his emotions. We try to share his compassion for all beings, his care, his concern, his will to heal. We can match this contemplation with action, doing things to benefit others.

The level of our ability to help them will be about as deep as our realization of our own true selfhood, so far. In order to help others on a deeper level, we will have to go deeper into ourselves—into the heart of Jesus and into our own heart. Ultimately we must go to the level of Jesus' realization of who he is, and when we do, we will come to a corresponding level of realization of who we are, remembering his prayer that we might be "with him where he is."

So, one must push deeper and deeper into Jesus and let him illuminate deeper and deeper levels of reality within oneself. Very strange things begin to happen as this effort progresses. We start out originally with the image of Jesus in his human form, but as we go into his consciousness, the outward human personality of Jesus seems to expand, as though one were in a spaceship riding into the sun. At the start of the journey one sees the sun out there as a disk, but as we get very close to it, it fills our entire visual horizon. Then we are inside it and it is all around us, and we don't see it as a disk anymore, out in front of us. Similarly, the human personality of Jesus expands and disappears as one enters more and more into the interior of his consciousness, and a complementary transformation takes place also in oneself as in a mirror image. What one *is* transcends what one *does* or what one *says* or what descriptive traits and qualities one *has*.

In this stage, which we may call the prayer of intimacy, what Jesus *is* communes directly with what one is, passing through and beyond the mediation of either's behavior or description. As the descriptions melt and evaporate before the burning radiance of each person's central reality, so the words that would capture those descriptions fail, and silence supervenes. The two luminosities gradually grow together.

Thus, by meditating on Jesus, on the one hand, and by repeatedly asking ourselves "Who am I, really?" on the other, we begin to renounce our sense of our particular personality, that personality that establishes itself in the world by its distinction from other personalities. And we renounce our pride, our sense of valuing ourselves as someone who is doing something good. We enter into Jesus' experience of himself as an instrument of God: God alone is good, and whatever Jesus does is really the Father's work. Jesus only does what the Father tells him to do, or what he sees the Father doing; or else it is the Father working through him.

This is the way he expresses his own experience, as he tries to describe to other people what it is like. Take, for instance, the time when he was on his way to the house of Jairus. You have to imagine a pressing crowd in the narrow streets. It's like going up the stairs from the subway during rush hour. People are pushing against one another, shoulder to shoulder. Then, all of a sudden, Jesus stops short, stands still, and starts looking around. "Who touched me?" he asks. Peter, not unnaturally, answers, "Master, the crowds throng and press upon you. Why do you ask, 'Who touched me?'" But Jesus persists. This wasn't like ordinary touching, he says. He could feel power flowing out of him. What kind of experience was that? It was the experience of being an instrumentality, whereby the healing power of God which was resident in him went out. He felt it migrate through him into somebody else, and he felt himself as an instrument of God.

And we too are called to become like that. We are to feel ourselves transparent, so that this light of the Source can shine through us. It is as though each of us had been a many-faceted crystal, painted over in various colors. We could see how we were different and separate from each other because the colored paint made each of us quite visible—by reflected light—as an object with definite boundaries. Now the power of renunciation—letting go our interest in our personality and our pride—dissolves the superficial decorations, washes the painted colors away, and lets the light shine *through* the pure crystal. When this happens, the crystal as such becomes almost invisible, as the light pouring through it floods out to the whole environment.

We not only do not take pride in what we do, we are scarcely aware of ourselves as the ones who are doing. We do not reflect upon ourselves in order to *observe that* we are leaving ourselves open to God's work and that such and so is taking place through us. We simply open ourselves and let our whole awareness be of God's life in and through us to whatever the work or expression of divine beauty and goodness is. The more we can make our eye "single" in this way and not let it divide into a double consciousness—partly on God's act of living and working through us, and partly a reflection on how well we're doing—the more our whole being, like the crystal, will be filled with the divine light.

In this way we gradually come to renounce our most fundamental habits of self-consciousness. This is the austerity that the mystic teacher warned was unavoidable. We have to be purified in order to be intent on God's Presence through us to the work. What we are is God's channel of activity, God's manifestation in the world. At this stage, the sense of being a distinct or bounded being begins to get fuzzy, because what and who we are is experienced as the continuity of God's activity in and through us, out to our neighbors.

Entering into the Subjectivity of Jesus

Let me propose another image now. It is the image of the Beloved Disciple, who "reclined on the breast of Jesus" at the Last Supper. Whatever that may have meant historically, I want to envision it a certain way in order to make a point about our interior attitude. I want to suppose St. John positioned with his back to Jesus. Jesus is behind John, not face to face with him. Therefore, when John wished to move closer to Jesus, for instance to ask him a question, he just leaned back toward him.

We do a somewhat similar thing in our consciousness—at least this is one way of describing it; it can, of course, be represented by all sorts of images and similes. In order to move closer to the heart of Jesus, we "lean back toward" him by sinking back into the depth of our own consciousness, sinking down toward the center of our being. This sinking is done by renunciation, drawn by the entrainment link we have made with Jesus, our having got into his "rhythm."

Each deeper level that we sink to, position our sense of "I" in, brings us closer to the heart or center of Jesus, because it is bringing us closer to our own center. It is as though we begin from the surface of a sphere and retract along a radius toward the center. At the center all the radii meet. As we move back and down and in toward our center, we are overlapping, so to speak, with the reality of Jesus more and more, as we come to corresponding levels of his being. That is to say, he and we are sharing more: more outlooks and attitudes, more feelings, judgments, desires and will, more self-realization. As we regress toward the center, we share more and more. We are *backing up into each other.*

The consciousness of Jesus, the interior of his heart, is becoming more and more "available" to us, "known" to us, "familiar" to us—because our own heart is sharing those same dispositions. We are coming to know the Sacred Heart from the inside, inside his consciousness, and inside our consciousness. And our "inside" is coming to be more and more coincident with his "inside." His Heart is becoming the heart of our heart.

The heart of Jesus is his subjectivity, his subjective consciousness. This is what he opens to us, but we can enter it only as subjects, in terms of subjectivity. We cannot know it as an object. And here is where nondualism comes in, because the last dualism to go is the dualism between subject and object. To say that we cannot know it as an object is to say that we cannot know it as *another,* as something that stands opposite us that we look at. That is why we do not face Jesus in order to move closer to him, but rather lean back into him. Were we to face him, we would always remain outside him. We do not look *at* him. You can't see a subject that way. "Looking at" would turn him into an object and you would see only the surface of his being, the outside. To know the subject, you have to enter inside the subject, enter into that subject's own awareness, that is, have that same awareness yourself in your own subjectivity: "Let that mind be in you which was also in Christ Jesus" (Philippians 2:5).

It is like receiving the stigmata of the crucified. You do not look at the crucified one; you yourself feel the pain in your own body. You become the crucified. Entering the heart of Jesus is like that. You don't regard the experience of Jesus, you become that experience. You yourself experience it in your subjectivity.

This is what gospel meditations are good for, and we can do this with many of these stories. It is especially helpful to take a story in which Jesus indicates what he is feeling, for example, the calling of Lazarus from the tomb, or the healing of the leper. The leper comes to Jesus and says to Jesus that all he has to do to make him clean is to will it. Jesus reaches out and touches the leper and says: "I do will it. Be made whole" (Matthew 8:2–3).

I once made a meditation on this scene with the leper in which I imagined what it was like to be the leper: to see Jesus, to hear his voice as he says, "I do will it. Be made whole." I heard him say that over and over, repeating it with him like a mantram, when all of a sudden I wasn't being the leper anymore. I was being Jesus. And then I felt this enormous will—"I do will it"—this huge divine will to heal. It seemed as though some great power, like a strong wind, was passing through me. And yet at the same time I was myself willing that healing take place. I was willing, it was my will, but it was carried and interpenetrated by that great will which came, it seemed, from somewhere behind me, passed through me, and pressed on to what it would effect somewhere in front of me.

These experiences, of course, are very individual and take quite different forms in different people. But the general idea of actually entering into the experience of Jesus seems to be common to them all. We can make similar meditations on what Jesus feels when he says: "With great desire have I longed to eat this supper [the seder] with you" (Luke 22:15). Or on what he feels when he stands on the hill overlooking Jerusalem and laments: "O Jerusalem, Jerusalem, you who kill the prophets and reject those who are sent to you, how often have I longed to gather your children like a hen gathers her chicks under her wing!" (Matthew 23:37)

If you keep practicing this kind of meditation, letting yourself enter into the subjectivity of Jesus, it will then become a question of how far you can follow him, back along that radius to the center, along the "road" that he himself is: feel the compassion that he felt, desire the salvation of the world with him, see the true meaning of creation with him, with him will that God's will be done, with him grasp that you are the Child of God, the manifestation of the Absolute Invisible Formless One, and with him realize that you simply *are*.

The Heart of Reality

When we come into his heart this way, then we know that he *is* the truth and that we *are* the truth: the coincidence of thought and thing, the union of subject and object, the interpenetration of "thee" and "me." This is the nondualistic experience. The reality one must know is, in this case, the consciousness of Jesus. One knows it by becoming it, by being it. We wanted to know Jesus intimately, and we have found him in the inmost recesses of our heart, at the center of our being. Found him, that is, not as another being, not as one whom we could look at, but as one who is himself looking out from our center.

After all, we must remember that Jesus' experience of *us* is a nondualistic experience for *him*, from *his* point of view. It is not only that we find ourselves coincident with him; he also finds himself coincident with us. When he wants to know us, he doesn't know us from the outside but from the inside, so that he experiences what we experience as subjects. Instead of looking at us or what we do, he looks at the world through our eyes and feelings and memories. He doesn't make us an object for his knowledge, just as we learned not to know him as object but rather as subject. God doesn't see us as something foreign, as an outsider. God doesn't stare at us.

Swami Abhishiktananda, whom I mentioned earlier, quotes a little verse composed by his teacher, Gnanananda, that says:

> *When I reach the depth of thee,*
> *Oh! What will happen to me?*
> *Oh! What will happen to thee?*
> *When I reach the depth of me*
> *There is no longer thee or me!*[2]

"In the abysses of the heart" to which we feel ourselves "inexorably drawn," says Abhishiktananda, "there is absolutely nothing" we can grasp or base ourselves on,[3] nothing more fundamental to which we can be referred. Did not Jesus say of himself that he had nowhere to lay his head? (Matthew

8:20) There are no more definitions by which our being is specified.

There was a road from our exterior, back through the layers of our being, into the heart. There the knower and the known coincided. We *are* truth. Now, together with Jesus, we realize that we are *life*. Traced back to our Source, we are life in ourselves (John 5:26). It is "the Father" who "has life in himself" and has given to his children to have life in themselves. In Abhishiktananda's words: "Nothing remains but being . . . being, pure light, undivided infinite light, light itself, the glory of being, the fullness of all joy . . . the Joy of Being, God all in all."[4]

> "Father, I desire that they also, whom thou hast given me, may be with me where I am, to behold my glory which thou hast given me in thy love for me before the foundation of the world." (John 17:24)

SEVEN

♦

The Communion of the Saints

J esus says to us, "Abide in my love." I am going to interpret this as not so much an invitation to rest and feel secure because Jesus loves us—although that is un-doubtedly true—as an instruction to *do* something. I am going to propose that this is another way of putting his new commandment "Love one another as I have loved you." To abide in his love means first to enter into his act of loving by entering his heart, and then to abide there, continually joining him in his activity of loving. We abide in *his* love when we love one another.

In other words, everything that has been said about coin-ciding with the interior experience and love of Jesus must now be applied to our relationship with one another. This is the meaning of the holy communion. It leads to the holy community, that is, the communion of the saints.

We need to dwell on the fact that the saints are present with us. When we speak of "the saints" we mean all holy people: angelic or human, dead or alive, of our tradition or not—all persons striving to become whole in goodness, truth, and love. We have, perhaps, to some degree lost this sense of the presence of the saints, not just the canonized saints but also the private saints of each one of us—family and friends, people we have known or heard about. These people are mystically present to us in the holy communion of saints: the deeper reaches of our consciousness indwells theirs and theirs, ours; at their level they become available to us.

Perhaps you have had the experience of being present at the chanting of a litany in which the names of many saints of a particular tradition are recited. It can give a wonderful sense of the "family" in which one lives, of the handing on of life from generation to generation, crossing centuries and millennia. In some traditions such lists are kept up to date, with new names regularly added. Sometimes the persons mentioned are not primarily "religious" figures but may be musicians, scientists, humanitarians. In our private litanies we can add our own heroes, relatives, and friends. We can include the saints of other lineages; they belong to us too.

This is our family in the spiritual order, the family of saints. And we also are saints. You may not think of yourself as exactly a saint, but if you are a sincere seeker after wholeness, then you belong to this community. I'm sure that not all the Romans and Corinthians Paul addressed as "saints" were paragons of virtue, but it was their vocation, and is ours, to strive to fulfill Jesus' command to love him by loving one another. We should believe in ourselves as saints. If we celebrate November 1 as All Saints' Day, we should claim it and enjoy it as our feast day. If we recite the Apostles' Creed, we should turn our attention seriously to believing in "the communion of the saints" and asking what that means.

What I propose to develop in what follows is the notion that this community of saints is an expanded expression of the Trinitarian life itself, that being made in the "image of God" means in the image of Trinitarian "community" life. And this in turn comes about because of the nature of God, which is self-giving love. It is because of the nature of love and the nature of personhood and the nature of freedom that *community* has the central position it has as the very root of reality. *Community* is how being, even Absolute Being, and therefore all being fundamentally *is*. It is not something optionally added afterwards. It belongs to the essence. To understand community, therefore, we must begin by discussing love, personhood, and freedom.

Love as Free Self-Giving

Self-giving is the core idea in any treatment of love and personhood. What do we mean by it? Sometimes, in human relations, it means to give time, attention, emotional response, intelligence, creative skill, and bodily activity to another person's benefit. Sometimes it means to sacrifice one's material life in order to save another. It can also mean to procreate and to nourish and to teach. In general, it seems to mean to give what one considers oneself to *be*, as distinguished from what one *has*, to give what cannot be *separated from* oneself: in order to give it, you yourself have to go along and be present—you can't send it by messenger.

Since we cannot "detach," or separate, what we give when we love, we must give the *whole* of ourselves. This makes us aware that we are a whole, a unity. That's why love is so integrating and why it, above everything, makes us "holy" (whole). Whenever we love, whether we love God or our neighbor, we must love with our whole heart, our whole soul, our whole mind, and all our might. Otherwise, it isn't love, because that's what *love* means, giving your whole self.

And then, love has to be absolutely free. That is, it cannot be the effect or result or consequence of something else. It is not determined, not necessitated, not done under compulsion. It is not caused. But not only that. Real loving, divine loving, is not even done *for some good and sufficient reason.* God does not love us because we deserve it, because we are worthy, because we are lovable. Nor does God love us because we are unworthy, don't deserve it, are not lovable.

I believe that one of the basic principles that Jesus taught is that God doesn't operate in terms of "deserving" at all. This seems to be the point of the story about the workers in the vineyard who came in at different hours but all got paid the same (Matthew 20). This policy was offensive to the workers, who were used to the idea that rewards are proportional to deserts. But the vineyard owner waves all that away, and replaces it with the notion of "generosity." The *least* that he gives is what is just in our eyes, what we would make a deal for as a quid pro quo. But that isn't really how he operates. His own context ignores the question of deserving altogether and treats everyone equally with "generosity."

In the Sermon on the Mount Jesus points out that God sends rain and sunshine indiscriminately on the good and the evil, and then recommends to us that we be "perfect as your heavenly Father is perfect" (Matthew 5:45-48). Be perfect complete, not partial, whole. Give freely without examining the "deserts" of the recipients. Anyone can love someone who is loving and lovable. But if you would live up to your heritage as children of God, you must not seek such a reason for your love.

All this means three interesting things. First, we have no ground for feeling that God doesn't love us because we're not worthy. There is no connection between being loved by God and being in any degree worthy or unworthy. Second, we may release our interest in, and desire for, being worthy, lovable, desirable. This has been a big item in our psychology, not to say our economic and social life, and has mostly made us very unhappy. Sometimes I think that we want to be lovable even more than we want to be loved. If this were not so, why should so many have a problem about believing that they are loved and resist just accepting that fact, still focusing on whether they are worthy or lovable? And why should well-meaning preachers feel it important to reassure them that they *are* lovable "in God's eyes," or that God "makes them to be lovable"? Jesus seems to me to be saying, "Forget all that. Stop being anxious about such things. It's unnecessary. My Father doesn't work that way." If we could really accept that, think what a relief it would be.

Third, when we in turn love other people, we must do it the same way God loves us, without regard to whether they deserve it or not. Please notice that this means that we are *not* to say to ourselves, "I love so-and-so, even though he doesn't deserve it." Or, "The X's are my enemies, but nevertheless I love them." It means that we are to *break all connection* between the notion of "deserving" and the act of loving.

We have now identified the basic life principle of the communion of the saints. That is what is meant by abiding in Jesus' love. Live in the kind of love-world he has created, the love-context in which he lives. Do it the way he does it. "Love one another as I have loved you," leaving out any regard for "deserving" or "lovability," either way. Don't classify people as friends or enemies, don't rank them according to their degree of lovability.

Is that so hard to do? Well, we're not used to it. We were brought up differently. It seems "natural" to us that we should love those who deserve it because they deserve it, because they attract us, please us. Anything we have got used to seems natural to us and we resist any alternative principle of feeling and behaving, calling it unnatural or impossible or undesirable.

But the contemplative life is precisely that life which examines those things that seem so natural, the life that presses against the boundaries of the possible, that questions and rearranges what is considered desirable. And when it finds a larger, freer, more truthful way, it releases its former mode without a backward glance. We don't have to be bound by what we were brought up to believe. Contemplative life is a search for truth, for greater meanings, for deeper goodness. The contemplative must be a person who has enough confidence in truth and goodness to let go what we were brought up to believe in favor of what spiritual insight reveals as deeper reality.

When we see other people doing these larger things, such as loving someone who "doesn't deserve it," we marvel at their ability to do something that so goes against nature (that is, against what we were brought up to believe). Nevertheless, most of us admire them for doing so and call them "saints," which shows that something in us recognizes that this is truth. This is important to notice. The "saint," in loving someone who "doesn't deserve it," is not operating in the realm of either falsehood or fantasy. We recognize the saint's act as "holiness," wholeness, being right—that is, correct, true. The truth is, our deeper self tells us, that love *is* independent of deserving, and all loving should be that way.

How can we help ourselves to do this larger and better and truer thing, to love without referring to worthiness? I have a suggestion. I think it may tie several things together, and here, having talked about love and freedom, we return to the topic I announced: I propose the Trinity as the paradigm for our own community life because the communitarian aspect of the Trinity is the central thing that this theology has to say about it.

The Trinitarian Community

Community and personhood go together. When we say that it is the nature of God to be person, we are saying that it is the nature of God to be community. A person is that being whose characteristic act is not only to be conscious of being and conscious of being conscious of being (an *enstatic* being), but that being who goes out freely to will the being and well-being of another person, to unite with that other person in that other person's sense of being, feelings, and actions (thus, an *ecstatic* being). Person is a subject (one who originates an action) who can so thoroughly recognize, acknowledge, and empathize with the subjectivity of another as to take up the stance of coinciding with the other's own subjective viewpoint. Thus person has to exist in community. There have to be others to go out to and join. Person cannot exist in isolation.

I want to develop this in more detail and apply it first to the Trinity and then to the communion of the saints. To do this I have to explain something I call the "I-I" relation. This is a step beyond the familiar "I-Thou" relation which Martin Buber distinguished from the "I-It."[1] In the I-It relation, we as subject relate to an object as object. This object is regarded as not having a personal presence of its own, not being an origin of free acts. We operate as though we are the only personal consciousness there, and our consciousness—knowing, willing, loving—reflects off that object and returns to us. We experience nothing whatever of the object's own interiority, its selfhood. The object has no "face" for us. It is possible to relate to human beings this way, but we protest against it because it fails to recognize the reality that is there.

We correct this error when we shift to I-Thou. Now we are "face to face," we say. Whereas we had talked *about* an "it," we speak *to* a "thou." One personal consciousness confronts another personal consciousness, acknowledging that it *is* another personal consciousness, capable of its own free acts. Each responds to the other in dialogue. In this way we receive something of the other's interior selfhood, because the other tells us about it and we listen, take it into ourself. But what we receive is mediated, translated into the medium of communication, encoded. We receive it through images, concepts, tones, glances, gestures, which we have to translate back into what we hope are comparable memories from our own experience.

In this sense, although we acknowledge that we are dealing with another subject, it is still *as* an object (where "subject" and "object" are being taken grammatically, as the originator of action and the recipient of action). The other is someone whom we can know and love, even as we can be known and loved by the other, but into whose own subjective reality we do not yet enter.

If we are to relate to the other subject truly *as* subject, then we cannot "confront" the other. We cannot *look at* the other, or *listen to* the other, or *speak to* the other. These interactions, which had been such an improvement over the I-It relation, are still not intimate enough. They still are subject-object relations. The goal of love, which is complete and total giving, is union. This is why the mystics say that the union takes place in darkness (nothing is *seen* as object) and in silence (one does not *listen* or *speak,* because the self-revelation is not mediated, as the I-Thou relation had been).

We must enter into the other and experience what the other experiences *as* the other experiences it. Instead of being "face to face," the two faces are superimposed, so to speak, both facing the same way, so that they look out through coinciding eyes and speak through coinciding lips. The activities of the two subjectivities are confluent and simultaneous, instead of being responsive, alternating, as in dialogue. Each of them knows the other from the subject side, in terms of the experience of actually doing what the subject does. And each totally loves the other by uniting with the other in this complete way.

This is what we were doing in the description of entering into the heart of Jesus, and this is the union properly called "mystical." William Shannon, commenting on Thomas Merton's experience and writings, puts it concisely: "In contemplation . . . the subjectivity of the contemplative becomes one with the subjectivity of God."[2]

Now let us see what we can say about God as such a mystical community. The Orthodox branch of the Christian church, as distinguished from the Western branches of Catholicism and Protestantism, views the Trinitarian Godhead as a dynamic activity of the Divine Persons. Persons, so to speak, constitute their unity by the very intensity of their love-acts of giving divine life to one another. They so thoroughly indwell one another through their self-giving love that they are completely united.

If we apply the notion of the I-I relation to this conception of the Trinity, I think we can say that it helps us to think about this great mystery. The nature of God is love. Love is the act of a free person, without motivation. Love is the total gift of self. Therefore, when a Divine Person loves "another" Divine Person, total self-gift is meant. The Lover "goes out" totally in gift to the Beloved. This is *ecstasy*.

The intention of the Lover is to enter into the subjectivity of the Beloved in an I-I relation, the most intimate and thorough of all interpersonal communions. But if union is attained with the Beloved's own subjectivity, it will be union with the Beloved's *enstasy*, the profound "standing in" what the Beloved, in absolute self-realization, is.

But, then, what *is* the Beloved? The Beloved is a Divine Person, therefore also a Lover, one who "goes out" in ecstasy to a Beloved. Thus the First Lover, when uniting with the Beloved, is automatically uniting with a Second Lover, and joins the Second Lover in what the Second Lover is doing. But what the Second Lover is doing is loving, loving a Third Person; so when the First Person unites with the Second Person, they unite in loving this Third Person.

Notice that it is only by doing this, by loving a Third Person, that the first two can actualize their love and *be* what they are, lovers. It isn't really *love*, of the total self-giving I-I variety, unless you unite with that one you love in doing what that one is doing. And if what that one is doing is loving someone else, then you do it too. Your act of joining in this loving of someone else is precisely *your original act of loving*.

It is not something you are obliged to do as a *consequence* of your self-giving love. It is the love itself.

Remember that this kind of loving is not admiring or desiring or enjoying. It's giving yourself to the other in union with the other's own subjectivity. So if the other's own subjectivity is engaged in loving a third party, *your* act of loving has to be joining in this.

Since the whole nature of a Divine Person is love, the First Lover is bound to find that what the subjectivity of the Beloved is doing is loving, and so the First Lover's love is realized only when joined to the Second Lover's act of loving the Third Person.

It has to be a Third Person. It won't do to join the Second Person in loving the First Person in return, because then the First Person's love act would not be verified as ecstatic. There have to be *at least three*. When the first two in united love give themselves to the third, they join in what the third is doing. But this again is self-giving love, since the third is also a Divine Person. Ecstasy goes out to another to unite with that one's enstatic self-realization, which turns out to be again ecstatic self-gift to yet another. This could go on indefinitely, but beyond the Third Person the pattern simply repeats, so Three Persons are sufficient to express the whole movement.

The beauty of this model for the Paradigm Being, God, is (to my mind) that it establishes both unity and differentiation, or distinction, simultaneously and by the same active principle: self-donative love. Usually we have one principle to establish difference or distinction, and another principle to establish unity or sameness. But love has this unique property that it necessarily *differentiates,* because it consists of giving yourself to another (you can't give yourself to yourself), and by the very same act *unites* what it differentiates, because the intention of love is to unite thoroughly with the beloved. Neither unity nor differentiation, neither sameness nor difference, neither the one nor the many has priority; and neither is reduced to the other. This seems to me to be what the great dogma of the Trinity teaches.

Holy Communion

This is what is being celebrated in the great sacrament of Holy Communion. Jesus prayed that we should all be one as he and the Father (and presumably the Holy Spirit) were one. Now we have just offered a way of thinking of how they might be one. Can we be one in the same way? They give themselves to one another. The Orthodox say they give the Divine Life to one another. Giving life to another is feeding the other. Isn't that what feeding means, giving life? The symbol of food is the symbol of life. And to say that you are giving your own body, your own life, as food to another, is to say that you are giving yourself totally in divine love.

The Persons of the Trinity, then, may be thought of as continually giving themselves to one another as food, a constant holy communion within the Godhead. Our celebration of Holy Communion on earth is an image and a worship of this. Ideally, it seems to me, we should practice it in such a way as to show the perfect mutual indwelling of each in each. We are called to love one another as Jesus has loved us. Therefore in the celebration of Holy Communion we should each feed each other in symbolic expression of our total gift of self to each other in fulfillment of his prayer that we might be one as the members of the Trinity are one.

They each feed each other, give life to each other; we should each feed each other, give life to each other. Jesus says to us, I give myself as food to you. Now *you* do this, too, as my memorial. If I can get all of you to love each other and feed each other, that will be a fitting memorial of my life among you.

This would mean that the ceremony and the sacrament of Holy Communion would necessarily become the core and the foundation of a holy community in which that mutual feeding was lived out in every sort of way. It would lead, in an unspoken, unorganized, unimposed way to a kind of holy "politics," or "way of living together in the *polis*," the city, the human community. This is the ideal of the communion of the saints.

Can we do such a thing? I think we can. Jesus didn't propose, and try to start, something impossible or something unsuitable for human beings. But he did try to start something quite revolutionary, something with a new principle at its foundation. He has a grand ideal, and if we pretend to take *him* seriously, we must take *it* seriously. It is not sufficient to be interested in him only for what he can do for us, create a religion about him and make him an object of worship. From *his* point of view, that is hardly satisfactory at all. "Not every one who says to me, 'Lord, Lord,' shall enter the kingdom of heaven, but he who does the will of my Father who is in heaven" (Matthew 7:21).

But it takes practice. First, we have to think that something like this proposal that human beings live together and feed each other in image of the Holy Trinity is what the world needs; then we have to resolve that we will try to re-educate our psychodynamic energies—our thought and imagination patterns, our feelings—to be open to deeper interpersonal appreciation; and finally, we have to practice the meditations and the new neighbor-love patterns in daily life, with great patience and perseverance.

Most of all, we have to make sure that we have really grasped his new principle and have seen how truly *radical* it is, how it goes to the very *root* of all our interpersonal relations. We must constantly question him and constantly question ourselves and our institutions, critiquing, testing, learning, creating. The more we understand it, the deeper it will cut. We must not be misled by the fact that many things in our traditions, in "the way we were brought up," are presented to us in the name of Jesus but do not exemplify his new principle at all. We must have the courage to see this and to adhere to him rather than to the convention.

The communion of the saints is a real possibility; it is open to us; we can enter into it, and we can help build it up, as Paul spoke of building up the Body of Christ. But it will take work and it will take daring.

The daring I include in the vocation of the contemplative, which I consider to involve repeated trips out on various limbs. The work will actually be based on our already present deep reality as persons. We will not be trying to construct something that has no foundation at all. If the Trinitarian paradigm should be correct, then our own core reality, presently overlaid by the selfishness of superficial consciousness, is already a mutual indwelling in all our neighbors. The mystics of all traditions have always affirmed that in the ultimate view we are all one: somehow each one's reality and highest good are intimately connected to each other one's reality and good.

What I like about the Trinitarian model is that it enables us to accept this without having to choose between the values of the individual and the community. In our usual way of thinking—not based on the Trinity—we tend to contrast the individual with the community and to believe that what benefits the individual deprives the community, and what benefits the community must deprive the individual. Using the Trinitarian paradigm, explained by the I-I relation, we can see why this conflict is unnecessary. When sharing the life of my neighbor is what makes me to be me, to realize my full potential as a person, then the more I benefit the community, the more I benefit myself; the more I fulfill myself as an individual person, the more I benefit the community.

Mystical union so understood does not cause us to disappear in some amorphous sea of generalized being. Each person continues with subjective consciousness of being oneself, being conscious, being happy. But neither does this personal consciousness prevent us from being totally united with one another beyond any distinction of subject and object. Like the Trinity, we so thoroughly indwell one another ("I am in the Father and the Father is in me") that we are perfectly united ("the Father and I are one").

What the mystics tell us, and what the contemplative aspires to realize in direct experience, is that this union exists now; we are already so united with one another on some deeper level, even though we don't, with our surface consciousness, experience it yet. This is why we still pray "Thy kingdom come, thy will be done on earth as it is in heaven." What is already real in the heaven of our deep reality and consciousness is yet to become manifest *through our will and action* in the earth of the more superficial layers of expressed creation.

The Mystical Rose

I have an image for this. When I first tried to explain the I-I relation,[3] I spoke of a pair of spotlights playing on a stage, each casting a circle of light, which gradually moved toward each other, overlapped a bit, a bit more, and finally coincided. Each beam of light could then say of that one circle on the stage floor: "It is I." St. Teresa of Avila said something like this when she described the unitive life: sunlight comes into a room through two windows, but in the room it is all one light.

Later, I expanded this image to include many persons, not just two. I drew a diagram of overlapping ellipses instead of circles; when I had finished, it looked like a flower of many petals, so I (somewhat facetiously) called it "The Mystical

Rose." (See Figure A.) A friend reminded me that Dante used the same image[4] for much the same purpose, which I choose to take as confirmation that it's a good one!

Each petal represents the total consciousness of one person, and the overlapping represents shared consciousness. The point of drawing the picture this way is to show that out at the tips of the petals there is no overlapping, no sharing. This is our usual superficial consciousness in which we seem to be quite separate and disconnected individuals, even alienated and alone. What happens (says my explanation) is that we have a kind of "short circuit" in self-consciousness. The full petal represents total consciousness., but our *reflexive* consciousness, our consciousness of being conscious— and consequently what we consider to be our "self"—takes in only the tip and thinks it is the full extent of our selfhood. (See Figure B.)

But if our reflexive consciousness could go a little deeper, it would find some degree of coincidence with at least some other consciousness. (See Figure C.) Could this account for "telepathy"? Deeper yet, we would encounter more profound levels of consciousness in many more persons—perhaps the realm of Jung's "archetypes"? If we became completely reflexively conscious,we would be aware of our overlap at the core of our being with all other consciousnesses at the cores of their beings. (See Figure D.) The "overlapping" is, of course, an I-I relation in which the ecstatic and enstatic mutual indwelling takes place.

Now, if this is how we *already* are structured and related, then we actually are in communion with all the saints at the present time in the most intimate way. If this is the case, then the self-giving love of a multitude of persons is pouring into us even now, offering us life, willing that we should be and be abundantly. All the saints, at the core of being, are finding and sustaining us with their own "body and blood," their own life and being.

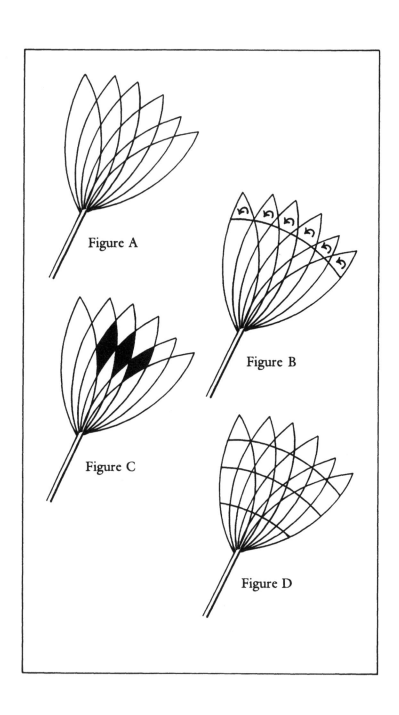

Figure A

Figure B

Figure C

Figure D

If we can believe this, if we can open ourselves a little to experience it, what consolation we can draw from it! And not only consolation, but a revised outlook on life. The affairs of the "tip" of our petal can be put in another perspective. We can see that the apparent separation is an illusion due to the short circuit of reflexive consciousness in the tip alone. We do seem to be separate there. But there is more to us than that. Deeper and deeper, we are more and more united. If we could look at life this way, how different everything might be.

Furthermore, with the knowledge (belief) that the saints are actually loving us—beyond all consideration of worthiness, remember—then we can relax our tense concern to protect and benefit ourselves. Ceasing to be uptight about ourselves, we become free to love others. We begin to make the cycle turn in the opposite direction. From a sin-begetting-sin cycle, it becomes a savior-begetting-savior cycle.

It is my suggestion that the contemplative life is directed to enabling us to become aware of this indwelling of one in all and all in one, so that we become sensitive to it and consciously active in that vast shared life. I believe we are called gradually to incarnate it and bring it to visible birth. The contemplative life is most truly the creative life.

EIGHT

◆

Trinitarian Manifestation

When we contemplate our world, we have to contemplate it through the medium of some model or paradigm. This is why we use similies, myths, parables, and philosophical systems. I have said that we should not identify ourselves with our descriptions but should try to realize that we are something much more than all our descriptions, something that transcends all description and definition. And similarly, of course, the reality of God and world transcends all possible description, definition, system, parable, myth, or simile that can be made about them. This was the point of the earlier chapter on the finite and the Infinite. The Reality itself—God, World, We—is Infinite, indefinable, indescribable, but we deal with it through the mediation of definitions and descriptions. We think of it in terms of models. It may even be that the way the Reality itself is set up is such that we are to use various models at various times, growing and evolving, expanding and generalizing. To use a new model now may not be a correction of an earlier model or the achievement finally of a true view, but simply an appropriate model for this particular age.

The Model of the Trinity

The model I have focused on is the model of the Trinity as the perichoretic process of self-donation through the I-I active relation. This gives us simultaneously process, nondualism, and highly personalized existential differentiation. There are echoes of ancient insights in this model. The nondualism comes from the Upanishads and may date from the second millennium B.C.E. The perichoresis arises from the New Testament and was developed in contact with Greek philosophy. The sense of personal differentiation has been growing, probably everywhere, ever since. The feeling for process as a fundamental reality and as explicit focus for philosophical consciousness, is both ancient Buddhist and recent Western.

In this last chapter I want to say something about how this model is appearing more and more as the general model of this age, and about how we can bring to manifestation in our world the ideals on which we meditate in our contemplative life.

One of the things which the model itself suggests is that the old dichotomies of inner/outer, interior life/exterior life, contemplative/active are obsolete. We now understand ourselves in terms of system, in terms of integrated processes, in terms of simultaneity, in terms of holographic presence of the form of the whole in every point of every part. Contemplation is a matter of realizing vividly, with our whole consciousness—intellect, will, affection, esthetic sense, and any other faculty we care to differentiate—the reality of our existence, of being here, now, in this world, in this God, in this community.

We don't have to stop doing other things in order to do that. It's what we should be doing at every moment of our lives. It's only in order to get started that one stops other activities for a time. Once the insight, the perception, the *sense for* that transcendent and full level of the whole Reality is functioning, then we can put back all sorts of activities without in the least dimming it.

In fact, it becomes obvious that all sorts of "activities" are the milieu of the contemplative act. Contemplation *is* hewing wood and drawing water; but it is also working in an office and teaching school. Let us not despise the activities of the present age and wish to be in some earlier era. We are not in the food-gathering world anymore, or the agricultural world, or even the industrial world. We are now in the information world, the world of human communication. Some of the communication is by means of, and even with, nonhuman beings, but they are thereby being drawn into the human world. We are leavening the lump. Humanness is spreading throughout the biosphere and the molecular and atomic worlds, and the lower levels of organization are participating in the meaningfulness that is the form of human community.

Even in our secular imagination we are coming more and more to view our world under the aspect of interaction and process. We see ourselves exchanging information and energy with all levels of our environment. So constant and so pervasive is the exchange, in fact, that instead of seeing separate beings standing at a distance from one another and sending messages across space, scientists and philosophers tend rather to sense one single organic whole within which the functioning parts relate to one another by simultaneous adjustment. This kind of process doesn't begin at one point and end at another. It is circular, and it neither begins nor ends. Every part or aspect of the whole is in intimate connection with every other part or aspect. "I am in you and you are in me."

Therefore, it is right and proper for contemplatives to be awake and alert to recognize what is going on in our world, to be able to discern the lineaments of the Trinity in the unpredictable gropings of evolving Nature. And if we have some grasp, such as is appropriate to us at our stage of development and under such images and models as are given us at this point, some grasp of how this vast being is the personal expression of the Divine Trinitarian Life, then we can appreciate it and work with it. United with a Creator

God, united with an incarnate God, we are engaged as contemplatives in the work of creation, the self-expression of incarnation. And we understand that what we are expressing is the Trinitarian Life itself.

Process and Interchange

Trinitarian Life appears in the simplest actions of everyday. It is in our material life. All matter is composed of extremely active processes and interchanges of energy. All our biological functions are exchanges with the environment of both energy and information. Sit down and attend carefully to yourself breathing. You are taking in air from the outside. It contains an oxygen molecule which enters your lung and gets into your bloodstream. It is captured by a cell and becomes part of "you." At what point did the oxygen molecule stop being "outside," part of the "environment," "not-you," and start being "inside," part of "yourself"? Having been part of "you" for a time, this same molecule may combine with a carbon molecule and another oxygen and be exhaled as carbon dioxide, after which it is again "not-you." This is typical of the world process. It is going on all around us, in us, through us, and *is* our life.

More and more our world is displaying itself to us in its essential character of intercommunication. News of the world is in our living rooms as it happens. We have feelings for strange people in foreign countries whose faces appear on our television screens with their human and understandable stories. As economic beings we are much more aware how globally interconnected our production and consumption are. The monetary systems of the world are intimately related and affect one another on a daily basis. We even influence one another's weather and must discuss with neighbor nations what they are doing to our rainfall or how their deforestation program is a threat to our oxygen supply. Not to mention how accidents to their nuclear power plants may affect our life and health.

A great deal of what we transfer to one another now is sheer information. Just being in communication with each other is a major part of our economic activity. We are sharing this work of communication with machines, and the machines are helping us realize that we are all living and working within *systems,* complex circles of circles of actions and responses in which each one's contribution is modified by each other one's contribution.

The notion of *system* is becoming a primary metaphor. We are moving away from the idea that some beings are put on earth to serve other beings and toward the idea that all beings share their lives with each other to their mutual benefit.[1] The world isn't divided into lords and servants, but is conceived by its Creator as a gigantic holy communion: "I am in you and you are in me."

Our ecological sense is taking an interest in such questions as the claim that all species are connected, for the production of gases, food, and waste removal, however circuitously, to all others.[2] And we are willing to ask ourselves whether the sum total of living things, the whole biota, is perhaps sufficiently unified functionally to act in concert to keep its earth environment in the moderate conditions that make its life possible.[3] We can consider the possibility that in the case of an ecosystem, the evolution of entities of higher complexity does not result from competition but from mutually supportive interactions among the constitutive parties.[4]

We are also studying the mathematical arguments that show that cooperation is a natural feature of an interactive system and that under certain conditions it is more advantageous than exploitation. We have been used to thinking of life as a "zero-sum" game (what one wins the other loses: positive gains and negative losses sum to zero); most of life is actually not zero-sum, but a game in which either all parties gain or all parties lose. In fact, cooperation is so natural that (when the conditions are right) it will evolve even among strangers or enemies.[5]

The Ecological Virtue

If we understand these things, we can work better in the world *with* the world. Instead of trying to exploit the rest of the world to our personal, group, or even species advantage, we can cooperate with all beings so that all live, all benefit. This is the *ecological virtue*. While Buddhists, Jains, and the American Indians, among others, have understood and practiced it, it may be something new on the moral horizon of many of us. We were brought up to believe that the rest of the world was created for our use and that the other creatures have no rights to life of their own. But the ecological sense should be an instinct in the contemplative, who should not have to stop and make a deliberate effort to conserve the environment or respect the rights of others. As participants in the creative act of the Trinitarian God, we should sense the great Whole as our own greater self. "Whatever you do to the least of these my kindred, you do to me." The whole world is the Creator's expressive gesture. God is in the world as the dancer is in the dance. The dance *is* the dancer, dancing.

Practice of the ecological virtue also means that Trinitarian Life should characterize our relations with other people. To contemplatives they do not appear as outsiders, as aliens, as potential threats to the deeper reaches of our being. The secret of their structure is known to us, and therefore we perceive that they are independent yet intimately present as members of the great We. Our sense of our own selfhood expands and includes them. The circuit of our reflexive consciousness comes home to a community rather than to a single isolated individual. It is like a vast marriage in which we can look at everyone and say: "This now is bone of my bone and flesh of my flesh" (Genesis 2:23). And "no one yet ever hated one's own flesh" (Ephesians 5:29).

Please notice carefully that this does not result in confusion. This is not a matter of blurring or merging; it is in no way like the state swallowing up the individual. That is the structural power of the Trinity. The Persons are quite independent, quite themselves, quite unique, perfectly free. If they were not, they would not be able to give creative love and thereby achieve that special kind of unity, the Trinitarian unity of freely shared life, in which the differentiation is as true as the union.

Notice, too, that in the human community the ideal is not exactly interdependence, though we often speak of it that way. Our life together need not be a matter of sharing our lacks, of filling up one another's deficiencies. We have for too long built our lives on the value system of deficiency. That which is in short supply is what is valued. We have even deliberately caused some things to be in short supply in order that they might be valued—not only material things, but things like honor, appreciation, esteem. We have felt that the only way we could perceive and value something clearly was by contrasting it sharply with something very unlike it. So we have tried to contrast ourselves with other persons, our nation with other nations, our religion with other religions. We can be right only if they are wrong.

But once we become capable of grasping the Trinitarian Life as the foundation of reality, this method of perceiving and valuing is no longer the only way to do it. We are now able to sense the reality of each person within the unity of the shared life, not as standing over against us but as being the one into whom we pour energy and will for abundant life and from whom we receive similar life energies. If we do not have to save most of our personal energy to defend our image-self by contrast with others, then all that energy becomes available to pour out on all others. We find we have abundance of being and value, and the more we share it with all others, the more we have, for our root-being as person is to be lover; therefore, the more we love, the more we are. The value does not come from being scarce but from being abundant and being shared.

The ideal for human community life is thus inter-*in*dependence, not the sharing of lacks but the sharing of abundances. And even now we actually *have* abundances; we can realize them as soon as we release the tensions of seeking to preserve our isolated and contrasted lives. Perhaps this is what Jesus is mainly trying to tell us: "I have come that they may have life in abundance" (John 10:10).

A New Abundance

We can actually have a whole new economy in which the ecological sense and the community sense combine to give us the abundance that we truly need for human life. Our notion of what constitutes "abundance" will no doubt shift, so that material things will become simpler, human and artistic things will become more central. It is also entirely possible that once we really *perceive* how all can be equally wealthy in the abundance of human life and once we really *will* that all shall be whole in this sense, then we will discover ways of providing also material goods without stint and without sacrificing our fellow creatures.

> "Therefore do not be anxious, saying, 'What shall we eat?' or 'What shall we drink?' or 'What shall we wear?' For everybody seeks all these things; and your heavenly Father knows that you need them all. But seek first his kingdom and his righteousness, and all these things shall be yours as well."
>
> (Matthew 6:31–33)

Learn to live, in your mind and in your feelings, in terms of the structure of Trinitarian Life, each indwelling each other, each giving life and love and well-being to each other; live this way, think this way, explain this to those you meet. If enough of us do it, such a pattern will become the paradigm for human consciousness. *Then* we will see what kind of economic system we will create. Let's not try to invent it beforehand and impose it on people. When we have changed in our hearts, it will naturally evolve.

People have thought that competition, the desire to get ahead of the other fellow, was the only motivation that would activate people to exert themselves and to strive for excellence. And *in our present mentality* and with the types of dictatorial and totalitarian experiments that have been attempted, there is plenty of evidence to support such a contention. But *once liberated*, the desire to give something to another, to make life right for another, to do the very best we can for another whom we love, is a far more powerful motivation. It needs to be released, of course, and it can't be released as long as people are tense with the anxiety Jesus was trying to allay: the need to protect, preserve, and augment our supposedly isolated lives.

Allaying anxiety is what Jesus is trying to do, I think. It is not useful, in my opinion, to represent him as threatening people with what will happen to them if they do not "accept" him or "believe in" him. That's no way to relieve anxiety and disperse fear. The one imperative that appears most often in the Bible is "Don't be afraid." We must first reassure people and relieve them of their fears. This is "salvation." Then they will be fit to give themselves freely to one another.

You can't successfully *require* people to behave as if they were willing to give everything for the Whole. People— most people—don't yet have any perception of the Whole as their own life; they don't have the natural feeling of *wanting* to serve their neighbors. They experience any such command as a tremendous oppression. Love can't be required. In spite of the language in which our tradition speaks to us, you can't really *command* people to love. Love arises originally and spontaneously in the very heart of the lover without any antecedents, including commandments. Love is the nature of being, of God; it is not something added on afterwards. Take away the damming walls of ego-defense, and the fountain of love will spring forth naturally and pour out without restraint.

This is why the abundance of "salvation" has to come first. *First,* learn to relax the ego-defenses by fully accepting God's unconditional sustaining love; *then* enter into the Trinitarian Life of shared personal love energies; and *finally,* manifest that life by incarnating it in the workaday world. To make this *last* step of unselfish behavior in the world, the condition for meriting the *first* step, the reception of God's love, is completely erroneous because quite impossible.

This is where we have made things so difficult and miserable for ourselves. We have tried to make ourselves believe that we have to do something that we can't do. This is why preaching against sin and punishing misbehavior have so little effect. They don't reach the root of the trouble, the belief that we are not loved, are not safe, don't have enough being.

Our most important task in the manifestation phase of contemplative life is, in my view, to correct this terrible error. We must preach and practice God's abundant, unconditional love. This is the truth of God's nature, the fulfillment of our own nature, and the rescue of our fellow beings.

Infinite Being at Play

This sense of abundance, and eventual manifestation of abundance, I believe, grows naturally out of our realization that the central being of each of us is transcendent of all descriptions, a selfhood that finds its home in intimate communion with all other selves, and that delights in joining all others in expressing the world in a variety of finite forms. We are not defined by the finite forms; on the contrary, we express as these forms. And it is just as much a divine act to express as a violet as to express as a sequoia. We must not make the mistake of taking these differences seriously as measures of the worth of the ones who so express. All of this variety of form is part of the divine life in its act of self-expression.

Indeed, it is a part of the divine creativity itself that it should express in limited ways. And that is the joy of it. The Infinite Being plays in the world by being limited. Limited being is a possible kind of being. Being always tends to be— to continue in being, to be more, and to be in every possible way. We ourselves, however, are not merely instances of limited beings on the periphery of the divine self-expression. In my view, we (in our true self, our deepest root), are at the center, with Absolute Being itself; we are united with the Infinite Being which tends to be, to be more, to be in every possible way. We are not merely the expressed; we are also the expressor.

Recognition of this is the important shift that contemplative realization brings. Released from identifying only with the particular limited being whose role we are sustaining in the great play, we can enjoy all the other parts, too. It is the Trinity itself, the divine interpersonal love process, which is manifesting itself, and *we are seeing it from the inside!*

In daily life this means that everything is transformed. The most familiar things and actions are shot through with the divine presence. Everything is marvelous, because everything is God's doing; nothing is ordinary or tedious or banal or trivial or unworthy of notice or care. Nothing is taken for granted, because everything is experienced as a gift, as a personal expression of a loving parent who is also a magnificent artist. And part of that artistry is to be found in what I do in my limited way. No work can be despised or begrudged. Everything is to be done as perfectly as possible so that God can truly act in what we do. In this way we act without tension or anxiety but with confidence, attention, and pleasure.

Take pleasure in everything you do. Always be aware. Whatever we do should be just like our sacramental experiences. After all, the sacraments are there to teach us how to have daily experiences, daily bread, daily supersubstantial transcendent nourishing experiences. And daily wine that rejoices our hearts. It is not only when one is before the altar that one can feel this joy. It can be experienced when we are doing whatever trivial or tedious task is the work of the moment. You've put on your alb (or apron) and taken candle (or pot) in hand, and you're going to the altar (or sink). Whatever you're doing, it is worship, it is divine expression, and it is joy.

All this is still contemplation. Contemplation is not something that is done alongside or before and after our everyday action. It's the doing itself that is contemplation because you yourself are so united with God that you are simply living the divine life; you are God living and doing *you* in the world. You are God's manifestation.

Contemplation was initially a movement of consciousness *from* the world, as we then were thinking of it, *to* God, as we were then thinking of God. Now manifestation is a movement of consciousness from God, with God, in God, *as* God, out into the world, a movement in which the divine consciousness and my consciousness, flowing together, stream out in love and in creative, healing, beautifying energy to create the world and to make it ever better.

We are now the Body of Jesus in our world, in our time, in our particular locality and historical circumstances. We are the Word of God made flesh. That is the consequence of the holy communion, the reality of the holy community, the communion of the saints. That Word has spread and extended Itself; the Vine has been growing branches, always more branches, and has circulated its own life through them. It has a mission: as Word its business is to speak; to make explicit, visible, manifest the Divine Goodness that transcends all speech. That mission is not complete. Jesus said: "As the Father sent me, so I send you. . . . The works I have done you also shall do. . . . and greater works than these will [you] do, because I go the Father" (John 14:12).

Jesus, being aware of himself as the Child of God in whom God is well pleased, comes to awaken us and convince us that the same is true of us. He wants to take us into his consciousness so that we can think and feel and will and see the world as he does and act in it as he does. And as fast as any of us is so transformed, catches the Jesus-consciousness, and is able to feel-think-see-will-act in that way, we are expected and empowered to pass it on, to communicate it to others: Freely you have received, freely give. We also are Word, speech, communication, transmission of truth and life. We also are rescue for those who are fainting on the road, exhausted by struggling with anxiety and insecurity. We also must say: "Come to me, I'll stop the pain. I'll give you relief."

Transform the World

Therefore, in our particularity and our concrete historical circumstances, our work is to see that consciousness transformation applies to our lives and to the world. No one merely experiences the world passively. We all contribute to the milieu which we and others experience, to make it better or worse. Our responsibility as extensions of the Word of God incarnate is to be attentive and intelligent and generous about our contribution.

Jesus talked a lot about "faith," or "believing." He said repeatedly that healing and forgiveness were "according to your faith." We make our contribution to the creation of the world in terms of our "faith." We believe many things about the world, about life, about ourselves, about the people close to us, about people in general. All those beliefs, those convictions, those images in our minds that we take for granted and on the basis of which we perceive, classify, and judge everything that comes our way—all that "faith" contributes to making our world. A whole host of things are being "done unto us," individually and collectively, according to our "faith."

Conversion is a matter of changing that "faith." We always have *some* kind of faith, some way of seeing and feeling about the world and our experience. Jesus sets out to help people *change* their faith, undergo a *metanoia,* that is, shift their mind-set, repent (think again), convert (turn around). The faith he wants to change is the one that sees people as judged according to classes, that lines them up as friends or enemies, superiors or inferiors, insiders or outsiders. The faith he wants to change is the one that sees a world of scarcity and hostility and insecurity in which we can't help being afraid. The faith he wants to change is one that sees God as distant or uncaring or threatening or rewarding and punishing.

We get the kind of world we ourselves create by our faith. The only way to change the kind of world we experience is to change the kind of creative consciousness we have, the kind of faith we have. It is our faith that creates the world.

Jesus wants us to have the kind of faith that characterizes the kingdom of God, to have that kind of model in our minds and in our imaginations, so that we will sort out our experience in those terms and bring that kind of world into being. Our actions flow from our attitudes, and our attitudes flow from our perceptions, and our perceptions are molded by our assumptions, our faith. Change the faith, change the assumptions, and the perceptions will change. Change the perceptions, and the attitudes will change. Change the attitudes and the actions will change. Change your faith and you will get a new world.

Get rid of the notion of measuring deserts. Replace it with generous unconditional love. Realize that God is "closer than breathing and nearer than hands and feet." Feel absolutely safe with God who loves us into being and sustains us always. Relax the need to grasp at life. Let go anxiety and trust, be confident. Recognize yourself everywhere you look and sustain this great self with full energy. This is the faith that overcomes the old world (1 John 5:4).

But we ourselves have to do it. The kingdom does not just float down from heaven. It is constructed by us out of our faith. It is always at hand, always ready and available. Any time we want we can bring it into full concrete reality. But it must be done collectively. That is why the program of Jesus, as a program for world transformation, has to be a community enterprise and not just a means for individual "salvation." Individual salvation is an atomistic way of seeing the community transformation. Jesus has prayed for each of us individually, that our "faith might not fail," and that when we have been "converted," we might "strengthen" our brothers and sisters, and eventually "be one" as the Trinity is one (Luke 22:32; John 17: 11).

This is why our work as the manifestation of God, the extension of the Word of God incarnate, is the culmination of our contemplative life. The goal of contemplation is to unite with the absolute Ground of Being, to join It in being and doing what It is being and doing. If It is indeed an Infinite which is expressing Itself as a finite world, then as contemplatives we unite with It when we realize ourselves as infinite and express ourselves as finite. And the finite is the image of the deep nature of the Infinite. If that is communitarian, then the manifestation will be communitarian. If that is based on grace and generosity, the image will be also.

Contemplation is a matter of seeing how it is, uniting with it as it is, and manifesting it as it is. How is it? We all have to strive to answer that for ourselves. I have shared some of how I see it. But I believe that the real contemplative never takes anyone's experience at secondhand. The real contemplative goes for original, firsthand experience. Contemplation can't, in the end, be talked about. It has to be practiced. There are people who have practiced and who have seen and who have manifested. "Ask, and it will be given you; seek, and you will find; knock, and it will be opened to you" (Matthew 7:7). It is a great invitation and a great promise. Let us accept it.

Notes

Preface

1. The expression "dancing the world" calls to mind, of course, the image of Shiva Nataraja, the Deity whose dance is the cosmic phenomenon. But I have two other associations with the words, as well. One is the fairly familiar figure of Aslan the Lion (C. S. Lewis, *Chronicles of Narnia*), who, as a type of Christ, sings a world into existence. The other is from Lyall Watson, who in his book *Lightning Bird* (London: Coronet, 1983, pp. 38–39) explains how the tribal people in Africa identify themselves with a particular animal whose spirit they express in their characteristic dance. Meeting a stranger, one asks, "What do you dance?" and the other replies, for example, "I dance the owl," or "I dance the jackal," or "I dance the snake." This characteristic dancing binds the community together and binds the community to the environment. It is in something of all these senses that I suggest on p. 126 that we "dance the world."

Chapter One   Leisure

1. Jeremy Rivkin, in *Time Wars* (New York: Holt, 1987), makes a distinction between calendars (which celebrate past events) and schedules (which are geared only to measuring limited time in the future). Classical societies lived by calendars. The modern world runs by schedules.

2. See Larry Dossey, M.D., *Space, Time, and Medicine* (Boulder: Shambhala, 1982), 49–50 and *passim*. The term "hurry sickness" was first used by Ray Rosenman, M.D., and Meyer Friedman, M.D., San Francisco cardiologists, in *Type A Behavior and Your Heart* (New York: Knopf, 1974).

3. Cited in Arthur Koestler, *The Act of Creation* (New York: Macmillan, 1964), 175.

4. "Abrahamic religions," i.e., Judaism, Christianity, and Islam.

Chapter Two   Stillness

1. I am indebted to the late Charles Inserillo of New York City for suggesting this distinction. His own idea ("Wish and Desire: Two Poles of the Imagination in the Drama of T. S. Eliot and Arthur Miller," *Xavier University Studies*, Spring 1962) is a little different, but I wish to thank him for provoking mine.

2. Discovered by Dr. Wm. S. Condon of Boston University School of Medicine, who photographed speakers and listeners, analyzed their "micro-movements," and found that the listeners' movements matched the rhythm of the speakers' speech and gestures. See George Leonard, *The Silent Pulse* (New York: Bantam, 1981), 14–17.

3. Letter of George Fox to Lady Claypole, 1658, in George Fox, *Journal*, ed. J. L. Nickalls (Cambridge University Press, 1952), p. 346.

Chapter Three   Meditation

1. Several pages on Coué, including a number of quotations (this one is on p. 35), can be found in C. Norman Shealy, M.D., *90 Days to Self-Health* (New York: Dial, 1977), 34–37. He references Emil Coué and C. H. Brooks, *Suggestion and Auto-suggestion* (New York: Samuel Weiser, 1974), a reprint of "Self Mastery through Conscious Auto-suggestion" by Emil Coué and "The Practice of Auto-suggestion by the Method of Emil Coué" by C. H. Brooks, but does not give page numbers.

2. Larry Dossey, M.D., *Space, Time, and Medicine* (Boulder: Shambhala, 1982), 3ff.

Chapter Four   The Finite and the Infinite

1. This triple identity is the central theme in the philosophy of Sri Aurobindo (Ghose), who speaks of the three "poises" of the Absolute: transcendent, cosmic, and individual. See his *The Life Divine* (New York: India Library Society, 1965) and other works.

Chapter Five   Sin and Salvation

1. Michael Flanders and Donald Swann's song "The Reluctant Cannibal," recorded in the late fifties on *At the Drop of a Hat* (Angel Records, S 35797).

Chapter Six   Heart of Jesus, Root of Reality

1. Abhishiktananda (Henri Le Saux, O.S.B.), *Guru and Disciple* trans. Heather Sandeman, Author's Preface, p. xiii.
2. Ibid., 105.
3. Ibid., 103.
4. Ibid., 103, 105.

Chapter Seven   The Communion of the Saints

1. Martin Buber, *I and Thou* (New York: Scribner, 1957).
2. William Shannon, *Thomas Merton's Dark Path: The Inner Experience of a Contemplative* (New York: Farrar, Straus & Giroux, 1981).
3. Beatrice Bruteau, "In the Cave of the Heart: Silence and Realization," *New Blackfriars* 65 (July/August 1984): 311.
4. *Paradiso*, canto 30, lines 115–30; canto 31, lines 1–12.

Chapter Eight   Trinitarian Manifestation

1. Even DNA cannot replicate alone but requires the aid of enzymes. Nor can the enzymes reproduce themselves but need the code in the DNA. See, e.g., Robert Shapiro, *Origins* (New York: Summit, 1986), 134.
2. Lynn Margulis, quoted without reference in J. E. Lovelock, *Gaia: A New Look at Life on Earth* (Oxford: Oxford University Press, 1979), 128. But see, e.g., Lynn Margulis and J. E. Lovelock, "Biological Modulation of the Earth's Atmosphere," *Icarus* 21 (1974): 471.
3. Lovelock, *Gaia*.
4. Erich Jantsch, *The Self-Organizing Universe* (Oxford: Pergamon, 1980), 106.
5. See Robert Axelrod, *The Evolution of Cooperation* (New York: Basic, 1984).

About the Author

Dr. Bruteau is a pioneer in the integrated study of science, mathematics, philosophy, and religion. With a background in Vedanta and Catholic Christianity, as well as the natural sciences, she has developed a broad, inclusive vision of human reality in its cosmic and social contexts. Analyzing the systemic and metaphysical roots of our social inequities, she offers an alternative worldview, featuring the incomparable value of each person and the community dynamics of mutual respect and care that follow from that view. This theme is developed as global spirituality, not limited to any particular religious tradition but accessible in direct human terms common to all.

Dr. Bruteau has published twelve books and more than one hundred articles. Her essays have appeared in journals such as *International Philosophical Quarterly, Cross Currents, and Cistercian Studies.*

Sentient Publications, LLC publishes books on cultural creativity, experimental education, transformative spirituality, holistic health, new science, ecology, and other topics, approached from an integral viewpoint. Our authors are intensely interested in exploring the nature of life from fresh perspectives, addressing life's great questions, and fostering the full expression of the human potential. Sentient Publications' books arise from the spirit of inquiry and the richness of the inherent dialogue between writer and reader.

Our Culture Tools series is designed to give social catalyzers and cultural entrepreneurs the essential information, technology, and inspiration to forge a sustainable, creative, and compassionate world.

We are very interested in hearing from our readers. To direct suggestions or comments to us, or to be added to our mailing list, please contact:

SENTIENT PUBLICATIONS, LLC
1113 Spruce Street
Boulder, CO 80302
303-443-2188
contact@sentientpublications.com
www.sentientpublications.com